Praise for *The Sales Professional's Playbook* by Nathan Jamail:

"Nathan's trademark comment "Living the Dream" has hit home with this book. His unique look at how the customer views the sales process and how to overcome those awkward silent moments is a work of art. The first chapter alone was worth the investment."

**Tony Rader**
Director
AUI Contractors, LLC.

"Nathan's straight forward, no-nonsense approach gives sales professionals an executable game plan for their daily activities and communications."

**Peter Patnaude**
Vice President
SRS Real Estate Partners

"Nathan has taken the Playbook to a new level... He breaks down the fundamental principles of sales into real sales tactics that will improve results in any sales environment."

**Steven Peters**
President
20/20 Companies

"This book is for the salesperson looking to develop and master the skill and disciplines necessary in the world of true professional sales. Nathan's book gives you not only the strategy, but also the actual game plan to succeed."

**Rodger Parker**
Million Dollar Club
RE/MAX DFW Associates

"Sales professionals can sharpen their saw by reading *The Sales Professional's Playbook*. Regardless of your level of sales experience, you can learn from this book."

**Jim Mickey**
Associate VP Alumni
Programs and Marketing
University of Texas, San Antonio

"I have served in the medical device industry for the past 22 years in sales, management and now executive management. Nathan Jamail has captured in a clear and concise manner the critical blocking and tackling basics of sales in any business. *The Sales Professional's Playbook* is a great presentation of the necessary skills that one must master to be a sales professional."

**Stan Dunavant**
President
US NeoTechs, LLC

"I've been a sales leader for many years, and I find the *Playbook* an excellent guide for team members desiring to become true Professionals. If you're striving to be a sales "professional," you will find this *Playbook* to be an excellent guide to success."

**Derek Bailey**
Sr. Director
Asurion

"Wow, this is great stuff. It has to be the best book I have ever read of all sales and marketing books. It's amazing reading, and I can't wait to tell everyone I know to buy it."

**Mark Regna**
Vice President
Jani King

"Nathan has done it again with his sequel, *The Sales Professional's Playbook*. I love Nathan's straight forward, no-nonsense approach to the overall sales process. Excellent core subject material – Bulls Eye!!"

**Ray Barnes**
Vice President of Sales
Extended Stay Hotels

"Nathan nails it ........again. Salespeople: be proud of who you are and what you do and never forget to practice. This philosophy is the recipe for success."

**Mark Brown**
National Sales Manager
Atrium Medical Corporation

"Nathan's done it again! He has simplified the art of selling and broken it down to the most critical elements. For anyone wanting to make more money and achieve greater results as a sales professional, *The Sales Professional's Playbook* is a must read."

**Wes Bowers**
Branch Manager
Delta General Agency Corp.

"My management team and I are big fans of Nathan's first book, *The Sales Leaders Playbook*. We found the approach can easily be applied beyond sales teams, as our production and engineering managers are following the program as well. In his newest book *The Sales Professionals Playbook*, Nathan's practical yet engaging approach is taking sales way beyond expectations. I believe buying *The Sales Professionals Playbook* is an absolute must for all professional sales people; in fact, it is required reading in my organization."

**Mike Leathers**
President of Hanson Engineered Products
Hanson Heidelbergcement Group

"What Nathan Jamail has done in **The Sales Professional's Playbook has knocked the legs right out from under some of the myths around what works in selling.** I love Nathan's no-nonsense approach to getting to the absolute core skills and strategies that drive sales success. **This book is truly a "no fluff zone" - with nothing but solid ideas that you can (and should) put to use immediately. Buy this book now and hope that your competition doesn't!"**

**Joe Calloway**
*Author of Becoming a Category of One*

"Nathan gets it—really gets it. The information he provides can be immediately acted on; it is sensible and it works. **If you buy only one book—let's make that two—be sure to purchase his *The Sales Leaders Playbook* and this book, *The Sales Professional's Playbook*.** You will be energized and immediately move into action to grow as a Sales Professional."

**Marian Staton**
*Vice President*
*Renaissance Learning*

# THE SALES
## PROFESSIONALS
# PLAYBOOK

Nathan Jamail

SCOOTER PUBLISHING, INC.

Scooter Publishing
2591 Dallas Parkway
Suite 300
Frisco, TX 75034

Edited by Kyle Cupp


Library of Congress Control Number – 2011902590
ISBN – 978-0-9817789-4-5


1st Edition
2nd Printing

Printed in the United States

# ACKNOWLEDGEMENTS

I want to thank my best friend, business partner and wife Shannon Jamail. Shannon is not just the greatest mother and wife, but she is my inspiration and my drive. Because of her support and help I have been able to take the many selling lessons that I have learned over the past 24 years of selling from my mentors, peers, clients and team members and create the playbook for my fellow sales professionals.

It wasn't until later in my sales career that I learned the difference between a sales person and sales professional, and to that I want to thank all my co-workers, clients and my family. Starting with the customer in 1991 to whom I was selling home stereos for HH Greg in Indianapolis IN, who told me that I should never say "To be honest with you", because it implied that I was lying the rest of the time. And to Mark Hood for giving me my first chance (or should I say sentencing) as a life insurance sale person. And today to all of the great people at the books stores who work every day so I can have the opportunity to share this book with other sales professionals.

Of course none of this would be possible without my mom and dad being the greatest parents a boy could ever ask for. They taught my two brothers and me about family, discipline and respect. I am reminded of this as I sit here writing this acknowledgment while my beautiful one-year-one baby Page is sitting in my lap saying, "Da Da", and my other two great kids, Anthony and Nyla, are preparing for us all to enjoy this life we love as a family. They are why when you ask me how I am doing, I always answer with "Living the Dream." Thanks mom and dad for starting this dream off so awesome.

I want thank Kyle Cupp for his great work in editing and help writing this book. And the great Noel Mares and the Trade Group for once again creating a great cover.

I can only end with saying that I know that I am not worthy of all of these many blessings that God has given me, but I am so very grateful.

# CONTENTS

# INTRODUCTION

In early 2007, I sat across a table from a potential client. He assumed a posture that spoke both of his hope and his concern. He was a homebuilder, and I don't have to tell you what was going on in the housing industry during this time. The stress of his being in charge of all of the sales departments throughout his organization weighed heavily upon his shoulders and showed in his tired eyes. His voice, however, remained confident.

The purpose of our meeting was for me to understand what his struggles were, and what areas of opportunity for improvement his organization may have. He cut to the chase: "Sales are down over 25%, and I really want to help our sales people turn this around." He had come to me for help, and I was ready to give it.

"What type of selling skills practice program are you thinking about implementing?" I asked, indicating at the start where I wanted him to go.

"Oh, my sales people know how to sell; heck, some of them have been selling for over 25 years," he replied immediately, not yet seeing the destination to which we were headed.

I decided to get to the goal with a roundabout detour: "If the problem is not your sales team's skills, then what do you think the problem is?"

With a soft sigh and a little less confidence, he said, "The competition is cutting pricing, we have too much inventory on the ground, the economy is in the tank and now the banks won't lend any money to potential buyers."

"Of all of those issue you named, how many of them can your sales team control?" I asked him.

"Well, none," he admitted.

"So, unless you are going to stop the competition from cutting their prices, or turn the economy around and increase overall home sales, or be the government and bailout the banks, then your sales team is the only thing you *can* control."

He agreed. I recommended that he think more like the coach of a winning football team, and less like a manager. I implored him to realize that his sales people should make up a team of professionals. They must learn willingness to change the way they play the game and never believe that they can be so tenured that they have nothing new to learn. Even the best of teams must remain humble, focused on improving, train and practice.

We put together a plan to do just that, and my client left looking no longer concerned, but ready to win. He saw the goal, and soon he and his teams made the plays and scored the touchdowns.

### BECOMING A SALES PROFESSIONAL

I have been in sales for over two decades. The last salaried non-sales job I had was a grocery bagger at Winn Dixie. I have sold everything from local newspaper subscriptions, encyclopedias at $1,000s a set, electronics, appliances, insurance, cars, pagers, wireless phones, mortgages, and real estate. I have spent several years in retail sales, wholesale, indirect distribution, business-to-business, door-to-door and Internet selling.

I don't share this with you to brag or to pretend I know everything; in fact, I believe the exact opposite. On most days, anyway. I share this with you because like many of my readers, I believe that if you are going to give expert advice, you need to have done much more than just research. You need experience and proven success.

I want lessons on hitting homeruns from an athlete who has hit lot of homeruns, not some self-described expert who hasn't swung a bat in his life. I am proud to say that no matter what my title or what organization I have ever been affiliated with, I AM A SALES PROFESSIONAL. I write about successful sales because I have been, time and again, a successful sales professional.

My hope with this book is to help you become a successful sales professional as well, but your success requires much more than reading this book. It requires that you put into practice the lessons it teaches. Throughout this book I am going to share with you stories, key activities and practice techniques that can help any sales person, regardless of the widget or service being sold.

What you will read in this book are my experiences, and I challenge you to consider whether some of these things can benefit you and your business. I often refer to one of my favorite quotes by Winston Churchill: "Personally I'm always ready to learn, although I do not *always like* being *taught*." This is an understatement for most of us. I know many sales people and leaders who say they are willing to learn and say they don't know everything, but deep down inside they truly don't want to learn anything and feel that they *already* know it all.

If this describes you, I share this one thought with you: the wealthiest and most successful people in the world are the first people to listen, take notes, try something new and different and continually search for new information. They are elite precisely because they know they can and will always be learning.

I mentioned the word "practice" in the previous paragraph. It's a word that you will read a lot in this playbook. Experience and insight have taught me that the world of sales and the world of sports follow many of the same rules. Perhaps the most important rule shared by both is the necessity of practice.

Imagine what would happen if the players of a successful football team suddenly stopped practicing and honed their skills only when playing the game. What you probably imagine is a perpetually losing sports team, and if so, you're right, yet this image matches much of the world of sales. Salespeople seldom if ever practice, but true sales professionals, like true sports professionals, practice daily. Your willingness to learn begins with your willingness to practice.

When you see a box like this, it signifies an important topic or relevant quote.

I hope you enjoy this book as much as I enjoyed writing it. The book reads like you speak, so it should read fast and to the point. In addition, the chapters are short, so we can get to the point and move on, making the book perfect for those of us with the tendency to drift after a few pages or who don't have a whole lot of extra time to try to decipher a complicated textbook of theories. Please enjoy and thanks for allowing me to share with you.

Now, let's take to the field.

# 1

# PROFESSIONAL SALESMANSHIP

Pro·fess·ion·al (prə-ˈfesh-nəl) adj. 1. *Participating for gain or livelihood in an activity or field.*

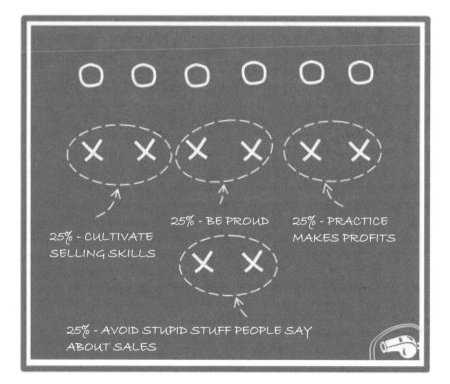

Welcome to the field. The game is professional salesmanship, and you're reading the playbook for professional sales.

Anyone with a voice and a smile can be a salesperson, but it takes a skilled, driven, and eager-to-learn person to be a successful sales professional. This chapter presents an overview of what professional salesmanship requires. The subsequent chapters will get into more detail about those requirements.

> There's a big difference between a salesperson and a sales professional.

Whether you are seasoned in sales or are just getting started in the business, this chapter will point you in the direction you need to go to become a top performing sales professional. First, you need to focus your attention on what professional sales really is by avoiding stupid advice people often give about sales. Next, you take a step towards professionalism by being proud of your profession. After that, you work on developing sales as a skill. Finally, you practice and maintain a regular practice program.

## PROFESSIONAL SALES: 25% - AVOIDING STUPID STUFF PEOPLE SAY ABOUT SALES

A lot of sales teams and their leaders misunderstand what sales is all about. Such misunderstanding often originates from their saying and thinking stupid stuff about the sales process. When I hear salespeople make overly broad statements such as "Sales is a numbers game" or "Sales is a relationship business" or, my favorite, "Sales is a people business," I get a bit annoyed. Hearing such statements is like listening to a coach try to manage a losing sports team with only nice sounding platitudes. Imagine such a coach telling his players that baseball is a game of balls and bats or that basketball is a game of jumping and concentration. That kind of generality doesn't win the game.

## JUST BECAUSE IT'S TRUE DOESN'T MEAN IT'S HELPFUL

All of these general statements may be true, but they are too broad and ultimately unhelpful. They do the players no good. In the same way, broad statements do not help a sales leader develop a sales plan. They don't give the team members anywhere to go, and they certainly don't provide a map for getting there.

## GETTING TO THE GOAL

Sales requires skill and strategy, not just heeding broad advice about making calls or being nice to people. Sales is about understanding who we are calling, what are we asking the customer, what energy we are giving and, most importantly, establishing positions of influence with the prospective customer.

It's about likeability, trust and influence. Sales is not a complicated process, but it isn't easy either. That is why 10% of sales teams account for the majority of sales in most organizations. The very top performers often bring in more money than the rest of an organization's salespeople combined.

Selling requires more skill than almost any other profession. You are dealing with intangibles such as emotions, egos, attitudes and situations that are outside of your control. And yet you must manage all of these like a master mountain climber scaling a peak amidst a violent storm.

> "A sale is not something you pursue; it's what happens to you while you are immersed in serving your customer."
>
> - Anonymous

Selling requires discipline, dedication, self-motivation, organization, the ability to gauge situations, the ability to read and understand a person's body language and position, the desire to be successful and the desire to *learn*. There's no ready-made formula to it. You are like a tennis player having to return multiple shots coming from multiple, unexpected directions. And sometimes multiple players!

Do you think hearing that sales is a numbers game in anyway prepares you for managing those multiple shots or scaling that stormy mountain? Think again.

So the next time someone tells you that sales is a numbers game, ask them what the number is so whoever is telling you that can call it and get a clue.

## PROFESSIONAL SALES: 25% - BE PROUD

In 1992 I sold life and health insurance in Indianapolis, Indiana.   It was then that I learned what, as a sales professional, I *really* did for a living.  Early one morning I was meeting with my boss to go over some proposals of mine.  I told him I had a great idea that would help me get more appointments and also make people more willing to listen to me.  I told him I wanted to change my title from insurance representative to "financial planner."

My boss wasn't impressed with my idea, and he was right not to be impressed.

He informed me, in no uncertain terms, that life insurance salesmen become financial planners about 90 days before they find a new job.

> In business, you are what you get paid to do. Sales professionals get paid to sell.

He said, "You get paid to sell life and health insurance.  You don't get paid to consult, and you don't get paid to review a person's finances; therefore, you are not a consultant or a planner."

He wasn't threatening me or subtly suggesting that I update my resume.  His point was very simple: if I did not sell insurance, I did not get paid, so I had to stay focused on what I was trying to accomplish.  Renaming my job didn't keep me focused on what I did for a living.  It distracted me from my real job.  By reminding me that I got paid for selling and should name myself accordingly, my boss kept me focused on what I *really* did for a living: professional sales. I learned to take pride in what I did for a living and why a clever name change wasn't the boost to my pride that I thought it was.

## WHO WE ARE

Over the last 20 years, my understanding of my profession has grown even more. I have learned that being a sales professional is something to be proud of, not just something to put bread and baseball cards on the table. We should not try to disguise the job of selling with names like "consultant" or "problem solver." That's not who we are.

A consultant gets paid for advice whether or not the customer makes a purchase, and a problem solver gets paid for solving problems whether or not a prospect buys anything. A sales professional may consult with a prospective customer and solve problems, but the sales professional *gets paid* when the customer buys a service or product.

> Sales professionals are proud of their profession: it helps turn the world in the right direction.

Sales professionals get paid for selling a product or service. This is who we are and what we do. When we do it well, when we sell the right products or services to our customers and clients, then we've done something honorable and socially necessary.

## A GREAT RESPONSIBILITY

Whereas a doctor is vital to a person's health, a sales professional establishes a relationship built on trust and influence and is responsible for helping people make some of the most difficult financial decisions. Sales professionals sell products and services that people need and that are best suited to them.

If you are a true sales professional, who has true passion for the job, you get paid to do what you love, and that's a great thing. The road to becoming a sales professional begins with being proud of doing what you love.

## PROFESSIONAL SALES: 25% - CULTIVATE SELLING SKILLS

While I've just said that sales is a profession to be proud of, the ego is an expensive liability, so get rid of it, and start investing in getting better. As I explained earlier, selling is a skill, and as such, improving it requires *practice*.

Selling is one of the most difficult skills of any profession, yet the concept is fairly simple. The greatest mistake most experienced sales professionals make is thinking that just because they have been selling for a number of years, they know it all and have no need to practice. *A sales professional is never too good or has enough experience that he or she doesn't need to practice.*

### ATHLETIC HABITS

Why does selling require practice? Because all skills require practice. If you stop practicing a skill, you lose that skill. A skill is a particular kind of habit or what the ancient athletes called a virtue. As such, they have to be cultivated through practice, or else the habits are lost. If you're not *in the habit*, you're *out of it.*

> It is not enough to know of excellence, to see it on the horizon. Excellence calls for unceasing pursuit.

The sales profession requires habits of mind, heart, and body: quick and informed thinking, a positive and encouraging attitude, and a warm and welcoming demeanor, to name a few. Every day, a sales professional is either developing these habits or losing them, either getting better or getting worse. There's no remaining static when it comes to skills.

What would happen to a basketball player who practiced scoring regularly but rarely practiced passing the ball? Such a player would slowly but surely become better at the one and worse at the other, and this imbalance would affect his or her game. The player would begin to preference scoring to passing and would shoot to score when he or she ought to have passed.

What will happen to a salesperson that never practices the skill of effectively asking for the sale? He or she won't develop that skill, and when it comes time to ask for the business, the salesperson will be underprepared and be forced to wing it. You don't want to wing it at any part of the sales process, but definitely not at the end!

Practice is vital to the sales professional just as it is for the athlete. It's the only way to cultivate all the necessary skills and fully prepare you for each and every sales call.

## PLAYING VERSUS PRACTICING

Now some sales people don't practice sales because that they feel they practice every day when they go on sales calls or are selling to people. This, however, is not practicing; this is playing the game. The difference is found in the consequences: when selling to a person one is usually not willing to try something new or take too big of a risk, fearing the loss of a sale. When practicing, there is no such risk.

Practice therefore avails the sales professional with risk-free opportunities to develop skills that may not be applied in every moment of actual selling. Successful selling may help the sales professional develop some skills, but only those that are actually applied successfully in the particular sale, and even then only to a very limited degree, as the goal of the sale *is the sale*, not the development of skills. In the sale, you're focused on closing the sale, not on improving your game.

> "An ounce of practice is worth more than tons of preaching."
>
> - Mahatma Gandhi

If professional athletes ever said they are not going to practice anymore because they have been playing the game for x amount of years, we would call them crazy. Yet that excuse is considered perfectly legitimate in much of the sales world. It shouldn't be. The avoidance of developing skills through practice should be considered just as absurd as it is when done by professional athletes.

## PROFESSIONAL SALES: 25% - PRACTICE TO MAKE PROFITS

If you want to take your sales career to a new level, regardless of how long or little you have been is sales, start treating your selling profession like a sports profession. Athletes practice 90% of the time and play the game 10% of the time. Most sales professionals practice less than 0.5% of their time—that is half of 1 percent! Now in sales we can't practice 90% of the time or we would never make a living, but we *can* practice two to four hours a week. If you are a golfer, would it be safe to say that if you were to go to the driving range for an additional two hours a week, your golf game scores would improve? Of course!

### PRACTICE LIKE THE BEST

Where do you start? Develop a practice program for yourself! Coaches of top athletes such as Peyton Manning, Brett Favre, and Jerry Rice did not have to tell these guys to practice. In fact, the athletes themselves would arrive early to practice, stay late, and would coordinate their own practice sessions with other key players. Do the same. Find a peer that you respect and create a practice program.

I play to win, whether during practice or a real game. And I will not let anything get in the way of me and my competitive enthusiasm to win.

- Michael Jordan

Remember to *focus* on the basics, not the trick plays. Spend one hour role-playing telemarketing or leaving a message. Work on developing new qualifying questions and role-play the sales call or closing a sale, etc. Work within your schedules. Just as in golf, you can't do this regiment for a few weeks and then stop. Yes, it is going to seem routine and sometimes boring, like hitting hundreds of balls at the driving range, but if you are going to be a professional golfer or a sales professional, practice is part of the job. If you really want to be a top performing sales professional, practice is precisely what you are going to have to do.

## EVERYONE LOVES SCRIMMAGES

Now, let's kick square in the mouth the 10-ton gorilla sitting in the room (and, for some reason, dressed like an umpire). Everyone hates to role-play, but, oddly enough, everyone loves to scrimmage. My kid's little league team jumps at the chance to scrimmage. When I played sports, I loved the scrimmages almost more than the games. Scrimmages seem like games, but they are really practices, and, truth be told, role-plays.

So why do we quietly shy away from role-playing, but excitedly run to the field for scrimmages? I have found the problem with role-playing is not the actual act of the role-play; rather it is the reason behind the role-play that causes the problem. In most businesses, role-playing is viewed as a way to see how much people know or how well they can sell; therefore, it ends in a judgment of results. This judging of results is the reason most sales managers do not make their sales teams role-play. They themselves don't want to role-play in fear that their sales people might see them make a mistake.

However, the intent of role-playing, what we will from now on call "scrimmaging," is to practice and try new things without real negative consequences such as the loss of a sale. A great scrimmage will not be a perfect routine sales call; in fact, it should have some new and creative twists. Have you thought about trying some new technique or tactic but are unsure of how it will play? Well, the scrimmage is the perfect place to give it a go.

I believe the sales team that has weekly scrimmages as part of their key activities and disciplines becomes a winning team of selling professionals. If your manager doesn't have you doing them, get a group of fellow sales professionals together and make it happen.

The difference between an amateur and a professional, besides the payment, is that a professional practices, whereas an amateur just plays and stays the same. Hence, in business today, we have sales people and sales professionals. Which one are you?

### Professional Salesmanship

If you want to take your game to the next level and deserve the name sales professional, then begin by dismissing all the stupid stuff you've heard about sales and embrace what you need to do to develop professional selling skills. Be proud of your profession, practice, and pretty soon you'll find yourself swimming in profits.

In the following chapters of this book, I will cover in more detail the road you must travel to become a top performing sales professional.

## CHAPTER ONE HIGHLIGHTS

- Selling is more than a numbers game or relationship builder; it is about skill and strategy.

- Do not disguise your job with seemingly clever names such as "consultant" or "planner."

- Sales professionals help individuals make the biggest financial decisions of their lives.

- Sales people usually practice less than 1% of their time, but should practice regularly.

- Professionals practice and get better while amateurs just play; are you a professional or an amateur?

# 2

# KEY PRINCIPLES OF
# INFLUENTIAL SELLING

Sell·ing ('sel) v. 1. *To exchange or deliver for money.*

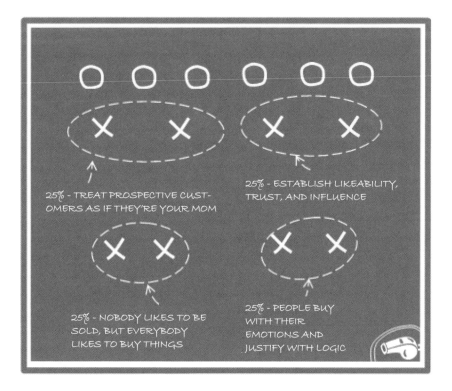

When I think of "old school" selling techniques, I'm often reminded of the cheesy 1980 Robert Zemeckis movie *Used Cars*. The comedy, which holds a place of honor in my DVD collection, stars Kurt Russell as a hotshot used car salesman named Rudy Russo. Your stereotypical "used car sales" antics ensue almost from the start.

Unfortunately, people often assume that sales professionals are professional liars. How did this assumption come about?

Early in the movie, Russo and his crew are getting piece-of-junk cars ready to sell, and they'll try anything to make a sale. Detached bumper? No worries. Russo takes chewing gum from his mouth and uses it to keep the bumper in place. High mileage? Not a problem. A quick turning back of the odometer plus a "low mileage" sign in the car window hides that pesky fact. Hesitant customers? Easy. The sales charlatans train a dog to lie down in front of a customer's incoming car, thus deceiving the driver into believing he ran over the poor animal, and then into feeling the inescapable guilt that can only be soothed with a purchase!

### THE OLD BUYER'S REMORSE

The movie is obviously fictional and full of exaggerations, but many people I know really see salespeople and the buying transaction as they are depicted in this silly movie. A friend of mine who is an engineer frequently comments to me, "Well, you know how salesmen lie." Sales and deception are synonymous in many people's minds, and not entirely without reason. *Used Cars* wildly exaggerates the sales process, but it is an exaggeration, the stretch of a truth. The jokes wouldn't be funny if they weren't based on some sense of reality.

Now it's not entirely the fault of the old school sales professionals that this regrettable stereotype developed. Sure, some salespeople, like people in any profession, lie like wannabe athletes boasting about their athletic prowess. More often than not, though, the stereotype of the deceptive salesperson arose because of a poor method of persuasion salespeople were taught. What I'm calling the "old school" selling method involved talking people into purchasing something in a way that led to customers sometimes feeling that they did not make their own choice, but were manipulated into making a decision to buy a product they really didn't want or could not afford. Hence the term "buyer's remorse."

## THE NEW INFLUENTIAL SELLING

In the past, we sales professionals would build rapport, ask open-ended and leading questions, and strive to overcome customer objections. The structure of the "old school" selling process is still applicable, but the *intent* of the process has changed. Nowadays, the intent of the process is not so much to talk someone into buying something, but rather to understand the customers and, starting from that understanding, to become a positive influence. Hence the concept of "influential selling."

Influential selling is based on four key principles:

- No one likes to be sold, but everybody likes to buy things.

- People generally buy with their emotions and justify with logic.

- Treat prospective customers as if they're your mom

- Establish likeability, trust and influence.

## KEY PRINCIPLE #1: 25% - NO ONE LIKES TO BE SOLD, BUT EVERYBODY LIKES TO BUY THINGS

People don't like to be sold. They don't like to feel manipulated. They detest being "sold" so much that the image of the used car salesman – the image of a manipulative salesperson that most frequently comes to people's minds – makes the slithering Jabba the

Hutt look straight as an arrow.  People who have been sold on too many occasions tend not to like, trust, or be influenced by salespeople.

## AN IRONIC SITUATION

Have you ever bought a car?  You drive to the car lot with your significant other, parent or friend, and as you are parking the car, you see him, standing by the entryway, smoking a cigarette, ready to attach to you like this morning's sweaty gym clothes. You say to the other person, "Don't look at him; don't even make eye contact, because he will try to sell us something!"  You say this, and yet you *are* there to buy a car!

Most people I talk to say that they would be happy if they could get a new car without having to go through the actual sales process.  I don't believe that to fully be the case.  I believe most of us like going to look at the cars and being able to ask expert questions, but we don't want to feel trapped or worry that at any moment we are going to be asked that great car dealer question: "If we could do X, would you buy the car today?"  We don't want to be SOLD.

## BECOMING A POSITIVE INFLUENCE

We as sales professionals want to give customers the opportunities to shop for things and buy things, but we also want to make the process enjoyable and the decision to buy or not to buy *their* decision.  *They should own their decisions as much as they own whatever they buy.*  Make no mistake: I am not saying we need less sales professionals or that closing the sale is not important.  I *am* saying that all sales professionals, even those who have been selling for 30 years, could stand to develop influential selling skills.  Being sold has a very negative connotation, which has given sales professionals a negative reputation.  Only sales professionals can change this image of themselves.  When done correctly, selling creates a well-planned, comfortable and structured environment for all involved.  By learning and practicing influential selling skills, we can

> When customers make the decision to buy, the decisions should always be theirs.

create the image of a sales professional as a reputable influence rather than a seedy character.

## KEY PRINCIPLE #2: 25% - PEOPLE BUY WITH THEIR EMOTIONS AND JUSTIFY WITH LOGIC

Over a year ago, my wife and I were walking through a store when she saw this kitchen table that she loved and just had to have. She tried discussing with me why we needed a new table. Our current table was too small. It was glass, chipped, old and so forth. None of these deficiencies had existed until that moment. I said to my wife, my voice dripping with sarcasm, "When we don't have a functional table, *then* you can get one." She smiled. And she seemed to agree with me! In my mind, my shot had resulted in a victory.

> "Confidence and enthusiasm are the greatest sales producers in any kind of economy."
>
> - O. B. Smith

I was so proud of myself because she agreed *with me*, and *I* had rid her of the new table idea. Or so I thought. Two days later, I got a call on my mobile phone from a guy who wanted to know if I would deliver the kitchen table that he just bought on Craigslist. Our kitchen table? On Craigslist? When did this happen? I called my wife for an explanation, still being polite but reasonably miffed. She calmly informed me that we no longer had a kitchen table and therefore needed to buy the one she'd seen and fallen head-over-heels for at the store. And so we did.

### LOVE AT FIRST SIGHT

My wife is like most people making a buying decision, whether that decision takes place business-to-business or business-to-consumer: people usually make a decision emotionally and then justify their decision with logic. When my wife first saw the new table, it wasn't the image of our faulty old table the first motivated her desire to buy it. She wanted to buy the new table *because she liked the new table*. I mean really, really liked it. It was only after this initial emotional response and the way her thoughts about the new table played in her imagination that she came up with reasons why we needed the new table. I had mistakenly thought that I'd shot down her reasons, but she was too clever for me.

It is the sales professional's job to get people excited about the product and service. When prospective customers are genuinely excited, they are more willing to make a decision to buy the product or service.

A brief aside: while the goals and ambitions present in business-to-business sales might be different than sales to individual customers, emotions still play a role. Don't turn off your excitement just because you're selling business-to-business. Consider the possible motivations of your prospects and why your product or service is right for them. Listen to your prospects to see what excites them. The possibility of a promotion, perhaps? New widgets for the company hardware? Build on their excitement.

You as the sales professional have to be excited and knowledgeable about what you're selling. You can't go through the motions or list off the product's features in a C-Span tone of voice. If you're not excited, you won't help your prospective customers to be excited. If you're dull, you risk dulling their enthusiasm.

Why? Because moods are infectious. Here's an experiment you can perform to see how moods spread from person to person. Go to your local fast food restaurant at the start of a shift, preferably during a rush when emotions are running high. Find the manager and watch him or her for a few minutes. Note what kind of mood the manager seems to be in. Now check out the crew. Note their overall mood. What you'll likely see is the crew's overall mood will pretty quickly come to reflect the manager's mood. If the manager is cheerful, the crew will be cheerful. If the manager is moody, the crew will soon be moody. Because the manger is running the show, he or she sets the tone for the operation.

As a sales professional, you set the tone for the sales process and for your customers!

### BEWARE OF FALSE AND FLEETING EXCITEMENT

You don't want customers to have a false sense of excitement or an excitement that dries up the moment they try to justify the purchase. The excitement has to be really theirs, not a feeling you're imposing upon them. The job of the sales professional is to influence, not to manipulate.

> Generate a whole season's worth of excitement, not just enough excitement for one game.

You should, moreover, help carry the excitement throughout the buying process and beyond. When customers leave with a product in hand, you haven't really succeeded unless you helped them get excited initially, helped them maintain excitement while they justified the purchase, and ensured they left your presence still excited and not the least bit guilty or unsure of their decision.

## KEY PRINCIPLE #3: 25% - TREAT PROSPECTIVE CUSTOMERS AS IF THEY ARE YOUR MOM

How often does your mom ask for your advice when making a purchase or before getting some work done on her car or home? Our moms, dads, children, siblings and friends can come to us for advice because there's no fear that they'll be sold. When we treat every customer like our mom, then we are sincere, honest and, most importantly, we help the customers to make the decision that best fits their wants and needs. We become a key influence in this little or big part of their lives. And the customers don't leave us anxiously feeling that they may have been deceived.

## ASKING QUESTIONS TO KNOW THE PERSON

Several years ago my mother called and asked if I would go with her to purchase a new TV from Best Buy. We went to the store together and were casually looking at some televisions when a young salesman walked up and started telling my mother about the various televisions and showing her the different features and benefits of each. After a few minutes of this, he told her which television he would recommend and why. My mother turned to me and asked me which one *I thought* she should buy.

Unlike the young salesman, I started to ask her questions, and because I knew my mom very well, I knew what was important to her and what questions I should ask. After going through several questions, she picked out the TV that was best for her.

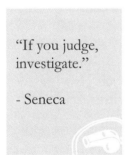

"If you judge, investigate."

- Seneca

I knew my mother and knew the best questions to ask in order to help her make the best choice, but I didn't necessarily have the knowledge of the products that this young salesperson had. While the salesman didn't know my mother, he could have and certainly should have asked her questions. How else could he have gotten to know her? He could have discovered her likes and dislikes, what was important to her and what wasn't. He could have gained that trust and influence I already had, and he was already more qualified to speak about his television sets than I was.

We often go with the advice of those who influence us instead of those who are most qualified to give us advice, and often this is a bad decision on our parts. Our family and friends aren't always qualified to offer us advice on what to buy or not to buy. I don't regret helping my mom make a decision, but I would have preferred that the salesperson assisting her acted as a sales professional and been an influence.

He may have been able to sell a television to my mom without such inquiry, but he wouldn't have ensured that she made the best choice for her. She wouldn't have left the store with the same excitement and certainty she felt after my questions and advice. In fact, I'd say my mom would have had more certainty and excitement if it had been the qualified sales professional, and not her son, who had been the influence.

The moral of the story: when we treat every prospective customer like our mom, we get to know who each customer is, what each one likes and dislikes, desires and doesn't desire. This personal knowledge of the customer should be our guiding star, not fact sheets and selling trends.

## WHAT ABOUT THE COMPETITION?

You might at this point be thinking: if I treat every customer like my mom, shouldn't I alert every customer to the competition's products if they would prove a better fit for my customers? After all, if I really wanted to help my mom or another choose the best product for her, I wouldn't limit her options to my products and services.

> If my product or service doesn't meet the needs of my prospect, I don't sell it!

Here's the thing: if I represent a major developer in an industry, chances are I have a product or service that meets my prospect's needs. However, if my product or service doesn't meet the needs of my prospect, I don't sell it! I give a referral or introduce my prospect to another sales professional, but I ask for a referral in return. I say, "You know what, based on what you've told me, what I have to offer isn't going to meet your needs. Let me give you the number of so and so who does. And if you come across anyone who can use my products, I would greatly appreciate it if you let them know about me."

# KEY PRINCIPLE #4: 25% - ESTABLISH LIKEABILITY, TRUST AND INFLUENCE

To be an influential sales professional, we must establish three positions with a prospective customer: likeability, trust and influence.

## LIKEABILITY

> Good energy, sincerity, and confidence lead to likeability.

People do business with people they like. Building likeability is a lot more about transferring the right energy by being you and being confident than it is about finding neat things in the prospect's office to talk about.

We're at our most likeable when we're out on the town, having a good time, enjoying one another's company, and being ourselves. We should have this same demeanor when involved in the sales process. When engaging with prospects, we should let our true selves shine through our words and mannerism.

The reason sales professionals should be themselves is that being oneself breeds confidence in who we are. We naturally act more confidently when we're not acting, and our prospects perceive us as more confident when they see that we're not putting on a show.

Moreover, if prospects like you and perceive you as confident, they are more likely to assume that you are competent. And if they assume you are competent, *they are more likely to trust you.*

Another way we establish likeability is by showing genuine interest. In my experience salespeople have a difficult time with this. They ask a few questions about the prospect's life, likes and dislikes, but then they promptly move to talking about the product. The prospect feels as though the salesperson was just going through the motions and is not genuinely interested.

When I ask questions to my prospects, I really want to know who they are and about the experiences they've had. Part of the fun of being a sales professional is meeting all sorts of interesting people with fascinating stories to tell. When prospects can see that you're asking questions because you really want to know about them, they'll most likely come to like you.

Finally, building likeability involves transferring the right energy and being passionate about your product or service. You're either transferring positive energy or negative energy, and being likeable obviously means that the energy you transfer is of the positive sort.

You never know what kind of energy and passion your prospects will have when they meet with you, so you can't leave the energy and passion to them. *You* have to set the energy thermostat and show your passion for the sales process.

When you are a positive and passionate you, genuinely interested in your prospects and in making their lives better, then you have earned the right to earn their trust.

## TRUST

Just because people like you does not mean they are going to buy from you. There are many people I like, but I would not do business with them because I don't trust their business knowledge or style.

It takes hours, days, weeks and sometimes months to earn someone's trust, and yet we can lose it in seconds. That's why honesty and trustworthiness must be habits, virtues, not just good deeds we practice here and there.

> Building trust is about asking the right questions in the right way.

We build trust in business similar to the way we do in life. We act in ways that are trustworthy. We keep our promises and commitments. We speak honestly and knowingly. We make it clear that we speak the truth when we open our mouths. Others know they can count on us to take the ball to the goal. *For the sales professional, building trust requires some extra steps.* Let's consider these.

> Expand your question beyond operational questions. Ask purposeful questions – questions about your prospect.

First, the sales professional earns trust by asking the right questions in the right order. What makes the questions the right questions? The questions are right when they are about the prospect's likes and dislikes so that the sales professional understands the prospect and can therefore recommend the best product or service for that customer. The sales professional should begin with broad questions about the prospect's company and move to more narrow questions about the product or service as it relates to the prospect.

Second, the sales professional builds trust by asking not only operational questions – questions about the features and benefits of a product or service – but also purposeful questions. Purposeful questions are geared toward three things:

1. What the prospect likes and dislikes
2. Proof of why you are the right one for the job
3. What will make the prospect successful

A key to asking purposeful questions is not asking them in a manner that has the prospect feeling interrogated, but instead in a way that feels to the prospect that he or she is interviewing you, the sales professional, for a job. The prospect feels as though he or she is in charge of the "hiring" process, and the sales professional can ask questions in a conversational and trust-inspiring manner.

Your prospects will trust you when they know that you really understand them and their needs, their likes and dislikes, what's in it for them, and that you care about all these things. And once you're a likeable you and have earned their trust, you're ready to become an influence and help your prospects carefully consider their decisions.

## INFLUENCE

There are also people I like *and* trust, but I don't view them as an influence. I don't consider their advice influential upon my buying habits and decisions. Why? It's not that they're bad or untrustworthy people; it's that they don't seem to have the right solutions or answers for me. I wouldn't seek their advice if I were making a large purchase, even if the purchase were within an industry in which they worked. I wouldn't want to be motivated by their advice because, frankly, their advice doesn't have the necessary foundations. If I wanted advice on hockey strategy, I would seek the advice of professional hockey coaches, not the observations of some untrained parent who watches his kids play the game.

> "The greatest ability in business is to get along with others and to influence their actions."
>
> - John Hancock

In a nutshell, influence requires a successful transition from asking questions to offering solutions and answers while, at the same time, establishing the value of oneself and one's company.

 The solutions you map for each prospect have to relate explicitly to the desires of the prospect. You do this by referring directly to what your prospect said in response to your purposeful questions. Listen to what they tell you in response to your purposeful questions. Whatever answers you give had better show that you were paying attention; otherwise you'll be stuck looking like that student who is daydreaming right up until the moment the teacher startles him with a question.

Being an influence also necessitates that you be open and up front about the good, the bad and the ugly of your product or service so that you're not overcoming objections from your prospect, but are helping your prospect to consider and make the best decision. When you bring up the pros and the cons, you are in the position to help your prospect consider the best option. If you don't bring up the negatives, your prospect will, and then you'll be playing defense.

## REACHING THE GOAL

Prospective customers must like us, trust us and clearly see our professional knowledge and our sincere concern for their happiness. Only then will they look to us as the sales professional who can give them the best advice when they make their buying decisions. Furthermore, when we become an influencer we don't have to overcome objections; rather we help customers consider their decisions. We focus on closing the sale, not on being right or being defensive about what we're selling.

Professional salesmanship is about the close – that's how we sales professionals get paid. However, it matters how we get to the close. We should be closing from the first moment of the sales process and at each and every step along the way. Closing the sale is like playing professional golf: there are a series of closes, but your focus always has to be on "this shot." You can't be thinking about the ninth hole when you're shooting the second. You have to be focused on what is right in front of you.

> Close the sale with each and every step of the way. Keep your focus on "this shot."

When you're building likeability, focus on building likeability. When it's time to build trust, focus on building trust. You close the sale with each and everything you do, so make sure you focus on each and every one of those things.

In the next four chapters we will examine specific practices that establish our likeability, trust, and influence and get into more detail about each of them.

Ready to break a sweat?

## CHAPTER TWO HIGHLIGHTS

 Old school selling was based on poor persuasion that created buyer's remorse

 New school selling is about becoming an influence and helping customers make their own decisions.

 Know your customer and know your product.

 A customer must experience all three virtues of influential selling in order to comfortably make a buying decision.

# 3

# INFLUENTIAL SELLING: LIKEABILITY

Lik·a·bl·it·y (lī-kə-'bi-lə-tē) adj. 1. *Easy to like; pleasing*

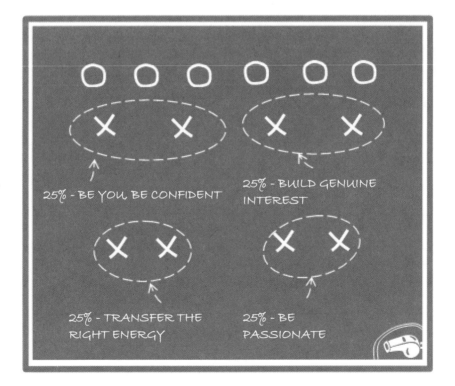

In old school business-to-business selling we were taught to find something in our prospect's office to relate to and use it to spark a conversation. The message was the same for door-to-door selling: find something in the home we could relate to and start building rapport. In theory, this lesson seemed simple and wise. Those awkward moments of silence are as harmful to the sales process as they are to romantic dates. Finding something—anything—to initiate a friendly conversation seemed like good advice.

In the field, though, the lesson proves ill-advised. More often than not, we come across as insincere, and our attempts at conversation feel altogether forced. Our ulterior motives are on full display, and our prospective customers are no more eager to "befriend" us than college jocks are eager to accept Facebook friend requests from geeks and nerds.

> "For every sale you miss because you're too enthusiastic, you will miss a hundred because you're not enthusiastic enough."
>
> - Zig Ziglar

We also run the unacceptable risk of saying something inaccurate. Sometimes our inaccuracies are minor. Sometimes they prove devastating. There's a story about a salesperson who went to a prospective client's office to sell his services, and while trying to build rapport, he referenced a photo on the wall of the prospective client. "Wow," he said, "how exciting was it having your picture taken with John Madden? When was that photo taken?" The prospective client responded, "The photo was taken last year, but that is not John Madden. That is my wife." Needless to say, the appointment ended soon after.

I know many of us have done something similar in our sales career. So what's the alternative? Instead of looking for a superficial object to use as a rapport starter, we can engage prospective clients in conversations based on *genuine* interest and personal involvement.

In this chapter we're going to examine what it takes to be a *likeable* sales professional. The plays we'll learn: Be You, Build Genuine Interest, Transfer Positive Energy, and Be Passionate.

# LIKEABILITY: 25% - BE YOU, BE CONFIDENT

I have found that people are more likely to connect with you when you are yourself than when you try to be someone else or something you are not.  In the sales process, you should always be yourself, unless, of course, you are truly unlikable, in which case I suggest you get out of sales and find a job that does not have anything to do with people.  A blogger, for example.

When on an appointment, act the way you would when meeting someone new at a coffee shop or restaurant.  Act as you would when you have nothing to gain and no ulterior motives beyond the enjoyment of the conversation and the chance to get to know someone.

## FROM BEING YOU TO BEING CONFIDENT

Being yourself comes naturally, so being yourself builds confidence in the person you are.  Being true to oneself and being confident go hand in hand.  When you act as yourself in the company of others, it shows.  You don't find yourself second guessing your words and gestures.  You don't panic after a significant encounter, wondering if you should have smiled a little more or laughed a little less.  You simply act as the person you are, and others perceive you as a confident person.

Salespersons who try to hide or escape from themselves appear much less confident in who they are and what they have to offer.  They come across as incompetent salespeople or as fakes.  Nice people, perhaps, but fakes nonetheless.  Exceptional actors can put on a convincing performance as someone they are not, but most of us are not exceptional actors, and when we pretend to be someone other than ourselves, our bad acting gives the game away.  Self-doubting fakes don't successfully sell products. They're not likeable.

> "Know thyself."
>
> - Ancient Greek Aphorism

## FROM NOT TRUSTING YOU TO NOT TRUSTING YOUR PRODUCT

If customers don't trust that you are who you say you are, then they won't trust that your product is what you say it is. They'll assume the praise you give of your product is false advertising, and they won't feel confident about making a purchase. At best, they'll say that they will get back with you on buying that new phone, flash drive, or flashy new car.

## CONFIDENCE IS KEY

Be confident! If prospective customers or clients feel you are confident they will assume you are competent. Of course, as sales professionals we must be confident without being arrogant. We must be assertive without being aggressive. Being confident is a balancing act of being sure of your product or service and of yourself while not being arrogant and causing the prospective customer to be distrustful or turned off. Your approach should be natural and effortless.

> Being confident equals people assuming you are competent.

Deviating from yourself tells your prospective client to deviate from you and your product. Being too showy or arrogant also puts you in a bad light; it's a huge turn-off.

Unfortunately, it's not always easy to tell when confidence ends and arrogance begins, and the line between them can be drawn just as much by how you speak as by what you say. What comes across as confident for one may appear arrogant from another.

A scene in the movie *Get Shorty* illustrates this. John Travolta's character, a loan-shark named Chili Palmer who's breaking into the world of producing movies, introduces himself to a potential investor as a movie director's associate. When the investor says to Chili, "You must bring something heavy to the deal," Palmer answers matter-of-factly, "I do: me."

Now such a statement sounds arrogant, but Travolta delivers it with such seriousness that he comes across as remarkably confident. You know he's speaking the truth and isn't exaggerating one bit. He's *likeable* when he says it.

Now I don't recommend you adopt Chili Palmer's peculiar style; you have to be yourself, after all. My point is that Chili appeared confident rather than arrogant precisely because he was being himself.

In a previous chapter I mentioned the importance of practice and scrimmaging and trying out new things. One of the things you can put to the test before your peers in consequence-free scrimmages is your style of exuding confidence. Your partners in scrimmage can inform you how they perceive you, whether you're coming across as unconfident, arrogant, or just right.

Remember: being yourself gives others the impression that you are confident, and being confident gives the impression that you are competent. And if your prospects assume you are competent, *they are more likely to trust you.*

## LIKEABILITY: 25% - BUILD GENUINE INTEREST

Do not rush when creating likeability. You'll strike out as surely as a batter who swings too early for every pitch.

Patiently ask questions to better understand the person you are meeting. Many times I find sales professionals will ask one or two random questions to the prospective customer and then go right into saying, "Ms. Customer, let me tell you why I am here…" Throwing out a few random questions is like tossing out a few lame pitches to a skilled batter. If your questions are not genuine and don't show sincere interest, then the prospective customer won't take you or your product seriously. Remember: the

> If you cannot name personal facts about your prospective customer, you have not earned the right to continue.

more you know about the prospect, the more likely you are to build trust. Take the time to prove your value before telling the prospect why you are there.

## GOING THROUGH THE MOTIONS?

In 1998 I was on a sales appointment with one my sales reps, watching him attempt to build rapport and ask questions about the prospect. It was obvious to the prospect, and to me, that the questions were not genuine and the rep was just asking them so he could get to the next step of telling him all about our product and services. Needless to say, the customer did not buy from us.

> If you're not interested in learning about your prospects, you cannot expect them to be interested in learning about your product.

I asked the sales rep what he thought of the appointment and he said, "I did all the steps. I built rapport by asking some questions, and then I told him about our product and continued to ask him qualifying questions and so on." Then I asked him to tell me three things about the person that we had just met. He could not name a personal fact about the prospect except for how long he was with the company he worked for. This rep did what many sales reps do: they go through the steps or motions, but forget the "why" of the sales process.

## STEPS TO GENUINE RAPPORT

Let me share with you some ways you can become genuine at building rapport and, as a consequence, move you a step closer to closing the sale:

Step 1: Write down questions you might ask to understand who your customer is.

Think now about the sort of questions you ask people you have just met in a social environment. Imagine you are at a party, a staff gathering, or a friend's birthday celebration. Picture yourself at a church function, your spouse's family reunion, or on a long flight sitting next to an interesting person. Entertain the idea that you're drinking a beer with your favorite movie star. What questions would you ask in these situations? These are the sort of the questions you should be asking your customers. Remember: it is all about *them*.

Here are some of my questions I ask a prospect when I meet with them, and I ask them because I *really* want to know.

---

### EXAMPLES: QUESTIONS OF GENUINE INTEREST

1. How long have you been with the company and in this position?
2. Have you always been in said field? If not, what made you change fields or careers?
3. Are you married?
4. Do you have kids?
   a. Boys or girls?
   b. What activities are they in? Sports?
   c. How old are they?
5. Where do you live?
6. Where did you grow up?

---

Step 2: Practice asking those questions.

Writing your questions down helps you remember, but it's usually not enough to keep them stored and easily accessible. Rehearsing the questions as you would a speech helps make the questions second nature to you. You don't have to think about them. You just ask them.

If asking the questions is second nature to you, then you don't have to focus on the words during the sales process; you can focus on transferring positive energy.

If you have to, bring the cards around with you so when you have a minute or two to spare, you can take them out and run through them in your head. Maybe you're waiting for an elevator or in line at Starbucks. Your day has these small pockets of time: use them.

So you have your questions memorized and have successfully used them in the field? Great! Keep practicing them! Vary them. Word them differently. Analyze and criticize your usage of them in the scrimmages and in the field. Revise them as needed.

Step 3: Ask these questions with genuine interest.

Remember, we get a fantastic opportunity to meet many individuals from all over the world, with millions of amazing feats, stories, and histories; have fun and get to know your prospective customers.

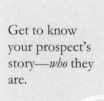

Get to know your prospect's story—*who* they are.

Each of them has a story to tell, a story they might like to share even with people that they've just met. People like you. After all, these days many of them likely share their stories to strangers through sites like Twitter and Facebook. We're becoming culturally less private and more open to others knowing the details of our lives. People are less guarded today than they used to be, a fact with potential for manipulation, unfortunately, but also with potential for getting to know more people genuinely—a real benefit to the sales professional.

The questions you ask help the customers tell their story, and their story helps you understand who they are. That knowledge helps create likeability and close the sale.

Step 4: Don't just stick to your memorized script: elaborate and go where the conversation leads you and the customer.

Depending on the industry or the job of the customer, I elaborate on a given question or answer. If a customer has an exciting job I will ask him or her to tell me a story about a memorable event. I once met with a prospect who was a former Navy Seal, and I asked him a ton of questions about his Navy Seal job, not so that I could get into a position to close the deal, but because I really was interested. I really wanted to know.

Because he told me his story, and because I was genuinely interested, I remember him to this day. When we as sales professionals create likeability through conversations of genuine interest, we become memorable ourselves, and I don't have to tell you why being memorable and likeable are beneficial to the sales professional. Okay, I'll say it: future sales!

By the way, I personally break all of the rules of what you should and should not say in a sales call, but this rule breaking is not for everyone. There is an old saying that you should not talk about politics or religion or ask too personal a question in a sales call; this is true as a general rule, but I am comfortable enough to break this rule. How much freedom to ask personal questions you should take is something you'll have to discover for yourself.

## LIKEABILITY: 25% - TRANSFER THE RIGHT ENERGY

As high school students learn in physics class or the football field, we are energy, and when we interact with one another we transfer that energy. The question every sales professional has to ask is, "What kind of energy am I transferring to others?"

> We are and transfer energy—good and bad.

Likeable sales professionals will be transferring positive energy, but of course positive energy isn't the only kind of energy one can transfer.

## THOSE DOWNERS

Do you know a person who displays and spreads negative energy? Such people say things like "I guess we can go to the movies, but the tickets will probably be sold out, the popcorn cold and the soda flat." They moan, "My wife is mad at me and my boss passed me over for a promotion. I never get anything. I have the worst luck."

Draining, isn't it? You want to hand them your cell phone so they can call a waaambulance. Do you hear a lot of energy-sucking statements? Are you the one transferring negative energy with your complaints about how life sucks? If so, STOP! Unless you're a Jack Nicolson character, you cannot be likeable by saying unlikable things.

## CONTROL YOUR ENERGY

When we are meeting prospective customers, whether it is in our own retail store, at a prospective client's office or at someone's home, we must give them the best energy we have. I don't mean an over-the-top fake and manufactured energy. I mean the positive energy you feel and express when you see a friend, or are joyfully hanging out with friends and family (the ones you actually like).

Make no mistake: you transfer energy to your customers. Make sure it's positive!

You cannot let a bad day or personal problems control your energy when you're in the sales process. What happens to professional athletes who allow a bad mood to fester during game time, who keep their scowl when they should have on their game face? They lose!

Moody sales people don't just fail to transfer positive energy to their customers; they succeed at transferring negative energy, bad energy that doesn't close the sale, but kills it.

If you want to get over the bad feelings or get rid of that bad energy, start by giving some good energy. You will get that good energy back, and that returned good energy will fire up your own.

Have you ever had a bad morning: you stub your toe on the door, spill coffee on your shirt, and drop your breakfast on the floor (which your dog promptly gobbles up) all within an hour of waking up? Then when you finally get in your car and head to work, you get cut off by some jerk and barely miss a collision. You're ready to give up on the day as surely as a fickle Dallas Cowboys fan.

But then you see or talk to someone with amazing energy, and your bad morning takes a turn for the better. Your day brightens all because of some positive energy you received from a positive person.

Here is a news flash for you: energy is controllable – it is all about your position and attitude toward circumstances and events.

If you want a prospective customer to be positive or have a good meeting, YOU set the energy thermostat. Don't wait for someone to do it for you because you might not like the energy you get. We are 100% energy, and when we use that energy correctly, when we have a magnetic or electric personality, we create a likeable environment and become likeable ourselves.

## LIKEABILITY: 25% - BE PASSIONATE

People follow passionate leaders. They take to heart the words of passionate preachers. They cheer for passionate athletes. And they buy from passionate sales professionals.

> "[Passion] makes all things alive and significant."
>
> - Ralph Waldo Emerson

In my experience, customers are more likely to buy from sales professionals who are passionate than sales professionals who are right—of course, that's no excuse for being wrong about your product.

Passion is a very powerful attribute. You can make a living doing just about anything as long as you're passionate about it.

Now you don't always have to be passionate about the product or service you sell (though you do need to have confidence in it), but you do need to be passionate about what you do for a living. I spent over 13 years in telecom, and I can say I was not overly passionate about pagers or wireless phones, but I was very passionate about sales and sales leadership. I was successful because my passion fueled everything I did.

Having passion for what you are doing is vital for building likeability. This does not mean you cannot be likeable if you don't have passion for what you are doing, but it does mean that you have to work a lot harder to get results. Passion fuels everything for us. It fuels our desire to keep going when the going gets tough, creates our energy and keeps us focused and confidant. It becomes the nucleus of who we are.

## LIKEABILITY IN A NUTSHELL

I don't want to over complicate creating likeability, but I want you to understand that building rapport and creating likeability has a lot more to do with who you are and how you do things than it is about what you say. I will sum it up in one sentence: Be a passionate and positive you, genuinely interested in learning about the other person and how you can make his or her life or business better, and you will be ready to start earning their trust.

## CHAPTER THREE HIGHLIGHTS

- Be you and be genuine.

- Confidence equals the assumption of competence.

- Take the time to ask the right questions.

- Selling is all about the *customer*, not about you.

- We transfer our energy, both good and bad.

# 4

# INFLUENTIAL SELLING: BUILDING TRUST

Trust (trŭst) n. 1. *Firm reliance on the integrity, ability, or character of a person or thing.*

Now that we have learned to establish likeability, it is time to move across the field, put on some new equipment, and earn the trust of our prospective customers. Remember, just because they like us, does not mean they are going to do business with us. We must *earn* their trust.

Think your customers will trust you without verifying your trustworthiness? Think again!

If you've seen the comedy *Meet the Parents*, you may remember Robert De Niro's character, Jack, telling his daughter's boyfriend Greg, played by Ben Stiller, about the sacred circle of trust and how he's either in or out. (Incidentally, the movie is more or less about the adventures and comic failures of Greg's attempts to establish likability, trust and, to an extent, influence). We as sales professionals need to be *in* the circle of trust with our prospective clients and customers. There's no standing part way in and part way out. It's one or the other, and unfortunately it's easier to step out of it than into it.

In my opinion building trust is one of the most crucial steps of the sales process, but one in which many salespeople lose the sale. They will limit themselves to asking two or three questions and then switch gears and make a recommendation, without having first stepped into the customer's circle of trust. Any recommendation falls on deaf ears if the customer doesn't trust the sales professional.

If you have ever taken any selling skills training classes, you have been taught to ask opened-ended and leading questions. I want you to take this training to the next level and take your sales strategy from the "old school" selling of *persuasion* to the *influential* selling process. Instead of asking *qualifying* and *leading* questions, ask *purposeful* and *understanding* questions.

This change is a lot more than just a name change; it is a change in principle. It goes back to the intent of the question. We need to understand *why* we are going to ask these questions and *what* are we going to do with the answers. In other words, our intention in asking purposeful questions is different than our intention in asking leading questions. They are asked for different purposes. Leading questions are aimed at leading the prospect to the product. The focus is on the product. The sales professional asks purposeful questions to better understand the prospect so that he or she can earn the prospect's trust and make the best recommendation for that prospect. The focus of the question is on the *prospect*, not the product.

When you visit your doctor, he or she asks you questions about your health or illness and, based on your responses, asks several more. Doctors ask these additional questions so they can give the most accurate diagnosis of your illness. As sales professionals we must do the same thing, but instead of diagnosing an illness, we want to discover what a person likes in order to build excitement, and what a person does not like so we can provide a solution. So what questions are we going to ask, and why are we asking them?

## TRUST: 25% - STRUCTURING QUESTIONS

I mentioned just above how a doctor will ask you strategic questions to diagnosis your illness. Doctors will ask questions that are somewhat arranged in categories. Each question helps narrow the search for the solution or diagnosis. The doctor begins by asking broadly about how the patient feels, next asks about specific areas of the body that are in discomfort or pain, and then narrows the scope of the questioning to the kind of pain felt and its duration. Is it as stabbing pain? A throbbing pain? An aching pain? This ordered sequence of questions brings the doctor step by step to what ails the patient.

Arrange your purposeful questions from broad to narrow; learn the general before you learn the specific.

We can see the same model of questioning at work in the selling of real estate. Through a planned series of questions, the realtor learns the state you want to live in, the city, the neighborhood, then style of the home, and then the amenities and so forth until the selection is narrowed to an actual home. The real estate agent would be terribly inefficient if he or she began inquiring about kitchen arrangements or toilet styles or even the desired number of rooms without first figuring out where in the world the Carmen St. Diego family wants to live. It makes no sense to be proposing homes in Fort Worth when the prospective client will be working in east Dallas. No, the agent discovers the big stuff first, next moves to the medium stuff, and finally narrows the choice by figuring out the prospect's preferences about the itty-bitty stuff.

Consider also the sales representative who sells lawnmowers. When a prospect enters the store looking for a lawnmower, the skilled sales professional will begin with basic questions and move to inquiring about specifics. Someone looking for a lawnmower obviously has a grass lawn and so the questions would probably begin by asking about the size of the yard, which more than anything will determine the type of mower (riding or push). The questions would then move to the type of grass, the design of the yard, the placement of trees and bushes, and finally to the preferences of the prospect. The prospect, for example, may be in the market for a mower that will provide more exercise than less, and so a muscle-powered mower might better suit him or her than a gasoline-powered one.

## BATTER LINEUP MAKES A DIFFERENCE

Your questions need to be crafted and asked in a logical, categorized order. Central to this order is learning about the customer. It's not enough to order your questions around your product or service. Your questions must inquire into the likes and dislikes of your customer. Too many sales reps learn all about their product and service, but fail to learn about their customers. If you only ask questions based on the product or service you are selling, you will find yourself stuck on selling based on price and customer service promises and not the customer's true interests, likes and dislikes. Start wide and work your way narrow. Let's keep it simple by breaking your questions down into three categories.

Category 1:  Learn about the Company

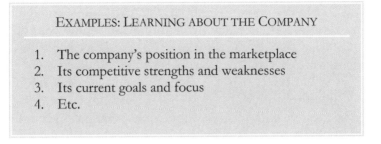

> #### EXAMPLES: LEARNING ABOUT THE COMPANY
>
> 1. The company's position in the marketplace
> 2. Its competitive strengths and weaknesses
> 3. Its current goals and focus
> 4. Etc.

Category 2:  Learn about the Current Relationship with the Competition

> #### EXAMPLES: RELATIONSHIP WITH COMPETITION
>
> 1. Who or what are they currently using?
> 2. If your prospects owned a company like yours, what would they do differently than their current provider?  What would they do the same?  What would they expand on?
> 3. What is the most important aspect of the product or service to them and to their company?  Why?
> 4. Etc.

Category 3:  Learn about the Product or Service as It Relates to Them

> #### EXAMPLES: PRODUCT OR SERVICE
>
> 1. How do they currently use this product or service?
> 2. How is what they are today good and bad?
> 3. If they were to improve any part of the service, how would they improve it?
> 4. Etc.

These are just some sample directional questions highlighting the importance of the order of the categories. You will notice that the questions begin by inquiring about the company for which your customer works, and conclude by inquiring about how your customer might use your product or service. The questions begin broad and become narrow.

There are hundreds of ways to ask these very same questions, so be *you* and be creative when you develop your questions. Have fun with it. Remember the more fun you have, the more fun the prospect will have with you, and the more likely you will be to earn the prospect's trust.

## TRUST: 25% - PURPOSEFUL QUESTIONS

When I work with sales teams, I find that most salespeople ask what I call *operational questions*. These are questions geared only toward the features and benefits of the product or service. They are questions about the product's operation or function.

> Ask more than operational questions—ask *purposeful* questions!

Operational questions will help you and the prospect understand how the products are currently used, but they won't help your prospects to know why they should buy from you rather than from your competition if the competition sells the same product. When you inquire into what kind of paper your customers use, how many pens they need, or what type of ink their printers use, you are asking operation questions. It is necessary that you ask them, but these questions alone will not lead you to the close.

### YOU HAVE ONLY ONE THING TO SELL

What? Only one thing? You may be thinking something like, "Uh, no, I have several products, and I want a high attachment rate for add-ons." When I say sell one thing, I am not referring to your product. I am referring, rather, to you.

Sales professionals have largely been taught to sell features and benefits of a product or service, and yet those same features and benefits may be found on a competitor's product or service. You can convince a customer to buy the product you sell and yet fail to get the customer to buy the product from you!

What's the alternative? Change your mindset from selling a product or service to interviewing for a job. In an interview, the person who is asking the questions usually has all the power and control over the conversation. Strange as it may seem, this is somewhat like the approach to take when meeting with prospective clients. Confused yet? Let's simplify:

In "old school persuasive selling," customers felt interrogated; they felt as though they were being tricked or trapped into buying a product. In "new school influential selling," a sales professional will give the power of the questioning process to the prospect. The sales professional will maintain the control of the conversation by letting the prospect know that he or she is there to help the prospective customer make the best buying decisions by understanding what the prospect is "hiring" for or looking to acquire. The prospect then feels in charge of the "hiring" process while the sales professional has gained a position to ask questions in a *conversational* manner. By "being hired," the sales professional is put in a favorable position to gain the prospect's trust.

> Think of the sale as an interview for a job. In doing so, you focus on selling you.

I remember several years ago meeting with the new regional manager for one of the major indirect distribution retailers who sold our product (as well as products of our competitors). I asked him questions to better understand what his thoughts and priorities were as the new leader. I told him my goal was to understand what his goals were and what made him successful. I explained that my team would like to interview for the job to be a part of helping him to achieve said goals. I knew that if I could find a way to help him reach his goals with our product, it would inherently allow us to reach ours as well.

As a result of my approach, this regional manager didn't feel pressured or interrogated by me. He felt as if he were simply participating in a relaxed conversation about achieving his goals and improving his business, which, of course, it was!

So let's put the process together and turn it into a part of the sales call. As we develop and ask these purposeful questions, I want you to envision yourself interviewing for the job to be the prospective customer's service or product supplier.

Please don't misunderstand: I am in no way pretending we are not sales professionals. As I said earlier, we don't want to disguise what we do with alternative job titles. We are selling. We make money when we sell. This process is about allowing the customer to feel comfortable with you, to trust you, and thus inclined to buy from you. By imagining yourself as participating in a job interview, your inclinations and actions tend towards earning trust.

Your purposeful questions should be based on three things:

1.  Learning what the prospective customer likes and doesn't like.
2.  Proof of why you are the right one for the job.
3.  Understanding what will make the prospect successful.

Make sure you bring your purposeful questions with you to the sales call. Have them in front of you for easy access.

I'll explain this further at the end of this chapter.

# TRUST: 25% - DEVELOPING QUESTIONS

The first step toward purposeful questions is to write down every possible thing you can think of that a customer may like or dislike about your industry, your company and your competition.

Take time to understand what the competition might be saying about your weaknesses and decide if you can transform them into strengths to the right customer. Pay attention to their advertisements. Visit the competition and find out. Doing this will allow you to develop questions that will help your prospective customer identify what they like and dislike, what they want to keep the same and what they may want to change. Things to keep in mind when creating these questions:

> Know what your customer dislikes, even if that which is disliked is a feature of your product.

- List *industry* weaknesses or common complaints (Example: Difficulty understanding the customer's monthly statement).
- What are some of your company's strengths? (Example: The most number of branch locations).
- What are some of your *company's* weaknesses and why does it have them? (Example: More expensive than most of the competition).

If you have a competitive disadvantage, bring it up for the customer. It is only an objection when the customer brings it up, but it is a point that has a pro and a con when the sales professional brings it up.

Once you have created your questions, test them. When asking the questions *you* must be able to answer the following:

1. Why they should by *from you*?

2. What are their hot buttons and points of pain?

3. What is their WIIFM (What's in it for me)?

If you can answer these three questions in concrete detail after asking your purposeful questions, then your purposeful questions have done their job. Remember: these three questions are for *you* to answer, not your customer. Let's look at each in turn:

## WHY SHOULD THEY BUY FROM YOU?

Understand and be able to communicate why you and your organization are better. Be specific and avoid the following four overused statements:

- o   Great customer service
- o   We care about our customers
- o   We are going to do what we say
- o   Our people make the difference

These statements are pretty much meaningless. Our people make the difference? What in the World Wide Web does *that* mean? Besides, difference isn't always a good thing. These questions tell the customer next to nothing about you. I compare them to similar statements people make when interviewing for a job:

- o   I am a people person
- o   I am a hard worker
- o   I am loyal, honest and dedicated
- o   I am a team player

> Be specific. Generic answers to how you're different just make you into more of the same.

No one ever says to a job interviewer, "I hate people. I am lazy. I'm disloyal and easily distracted. I am all about me and I don't know what *team* means." Not even Randy Moss or John Rocker.

You have to be specific and concrete when explaining why people should buy from you. You may not know right off the bat what the precise differences are between you and the competition, but you had better find out before your prospective customer decides to leave. Find out what your prospective customer is currently experiencing and you'll have a standard to measure your differences. Inquire about concrete details so you can provide concrete details about why the prospect should buy from you.

In addition to *telling* prospective customers how you are different, you can *show* them how you are different by how you conduct your sales process. If you build likeability, trust, and influence in the sales process, you're sure to stand above the mediocre salesperson with whom your prospects are too much used to dealing.

### THREE HOT BUTTONS AND THREE POINTS OF PAIN

If you have been in sales any length of time, you are probably familiar with hot buttons and points of pain, but let me explain these concepts anyway. When developing your purposeful questions, you want to discover three things a prospective customer likes and three things that are causing the prospective customer pain.

It is important to understand three things the customer is excited about, that they get emotionally attached to, that they desire in their products and/or services. These are their hot buttons.

It is also important to understand what frustrates them, what they wish they didn't have to deal with, or what they really hate. These are their points of pain. If you can eliminate these points of pain, they will be more likely to make a decision quickly and in your favor.

> Pain motivates, but not so much as solutions to pain.

Bringing up their points of pain doesn't work against you, not if you do it correctly. You don't want your customers dwelling on the negative, but you do want them cognizant of what ails them so they'll recognize that you have the remedy they need.

Your customers may not even be fully conscious of their points of pain. Consider that people tend to buy health insurance and especially life insurance later than they should. What happens? They experience pain or witness the pain of another. A sick friend. A deceased acquaintance. Suddenly they're thinking of themselves as ill or deceased, and they realize that they need to get insurance coverage pronto, even if it means a short term financial inconvenience.

It's your job as the sales professional to identify points of pain so you can help your customer make the best decisions and see the benefits of the long-term gain as preferable to the cost of the short-term inconvenience.

We make almost all decisions in life in order to eliminate or to avoid pain. By eliminating the points of pain your customers feel, you give them no reason to procrastinate and a good reason to make a buying decision quickly. You've cleared their way to the finish line and given them that extra burst of energy.

Now let's move to the next section, which covers the third question *you* should be able to answer: the WIIFM.

## TRUST: 25% - UNDERSTANDING YOUR CUSTOMER

Sometimes the particular benefits our service or product provides are not directly beneficial to the person to whom we are speaking. Moreover, the same feature may benefit people in the organization differently. Sales professionals have to be conscious of the WIIFM (What's In It For Me) for each person.

One of my clients sells educational tools and testing programs to help children learn more effectively and improve their grades and knowledge. It is a very noble product, but selling it is no different than selling a telecom service to a major corporation. Noble products and services don't sell themselves. Even the most benevolent of

# 5

# INFLUENCE: MAPPING SOLUTIONS

so·lu·tion (sə-'lü-shən) n. 1. *The process of solving a problem*

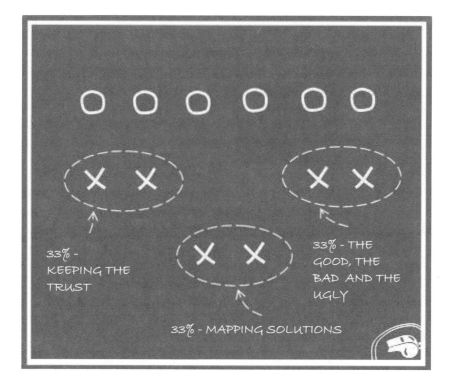

Your prospective customers like you, they trust you, and now it's time they are influenced by you. If you are thinking that this stage presents the most difficult challenge so far, you are correct. You are *so* correct. Not only do you have to succeed at what it takes to influence your customers, you have to remain a likeable and trustworthy sales professional all the while. You may have obstacles and hindrances coming at you from every direction as you race toward closing the sale, but now is no time to fumble likeability and trust. You can't reach the goal without them.

> "Everyone lives by selling something."
>
> - Robert Louis Stevenson

What does it mean to be an influencer? To answer this, let me, by way of analogy, call to your mind the profession of movie reviewer. The reviewer of movies is somewhat like a sales professional, but also very different in ways that matter. Whereas the sales professional gets paid for selling products that are a good fit for the customer, the movie reviewer gets paid whether or not people flock to the movies he or she loves or people avoid films he or she reviews negatively. The sales of the movie mean pretty much nothing to the reviewer, at least financially speaking. Nonetheless, to succeed in the long run, a movie reviewer has to be likeable, trustworthy, and influential.

To explain: the reviewer won't build or maintain a readership by writing with atrocious grammar, hackneyed expressions, or otherwise unlikeable prose. No one will take the reviewer seriously if the reviewer isn't trustworthy enough to give honest assessments of the aesthetic quality of films. To be likeable, the reviewer has to have something substantial to say about movies and say it well. To be trustworthy, the reviewer has to give unbiased reviews

To be influential, and this is the key, the reviewer has to get to the celebrated point where he or she shapes the way readers think about movies and impacts the sort of films they see and don't see. If a movie critic can influence a reader to see or avoid a particular film, then he or she is really doing the job. The best reviewers have their audience in mind when reviewing and allow their audience to affect what they have to say.

As a sales professional, you influence your customers when you influence their thinking and help shape their decisions about your products and service—specifically when you help them make the decision to buy or not to buy based on what is a good fit for them. This task is a bit more difficult than the film reviewer's job, as the reviewer has no stake in the movie he or she tells you to avoid, whereas you the sales professional need to sell the product or service to make ends meet, but you also need to tell a prospect not to buy the product or service when it isn't a right fit. Why this is the case we'll get into more at the end of this chapter and in the next.

First, the basics: How do you influence? How do you become an influencer?

We'll be covering the topic of influence in this chapter and the next. In this chapter we will go over keeping the trust, mapping solutions, and drawing attention to the good, the bad and the ugly (and why such attention is important).

## INFLUENCE: 33% - KEEPING THE TRUST

It can take hours, weeks and even months to build trust, but that trust can be lost faster than a triple play ends an inning. You can ask all the right purposeful questions, understand the prospect as best as you reasonably can, have succeeded in earning that prospective customer's trust, and yet lose that trust and lose the sale by failing to be an influence.

> Where the seeds of trust are planted, the tree of influence can grow.

Just as getting from one base to the next in the game of baseball has its risks, transitioning from asking purposeful questions (building trust) to proposing a solution (being an influencer) has its dangers as well. Whereas leaving 3$^{rd}$ base too early can get you out, trying to offer a solution too soon can cause you to lose the prospective customer's trust. If you don't have a great understanding of your customer, or ignore that understanding in favor of your preferences, you won't carry the trust far without a fumble, tackle, or pile-on. Getting your prospective customer's trust is like getting the football. It's a success, but you still have to carry it to the end, to the touchdown, to the close of the sale.

## TRANSITION WITH CLEAR INTENTION

There's no definitive step-by-step play that will always successfully guide your transition from building trust to making an accurate recommendation. There's no always-usable formula of words for it. Nevertheless, every transitional play you make must be a change of *intention*: your intent in asking purposeful questions is different than your intent in making a recommendation.

The step from earning trust to influencing is taken with switch of intent.

If you don't change your intent from building trust to becoming an influencer for your prospect, then you won't succeed in maintaining and building on that trust. Catching the ball and running with it are very different acts, but there's a moment between them where one transitions to the other. Making that transition, in sales as in sports, requires grace, knowledge and prudence. The key to making the switch is switching your intention.

# INFLUENCE: 33% - MAPPING SOLUTIONS

There are several things to keep in mind when mapping solutions back to the customer's likes and dislikes.

First, when responding to the answers your prospect gives to your purposeful questions, begin every recommended solution with an expression referring directly and explicitly to statements made by your prospect. Use openers such as "Given your concern about X," "As you mentioned earlier" or "Based upon what you said." Clauses such as these make the solution you offer all about *the prospect*. Yes, you're talking about your product or service, but you do so in a clear-as-day relation to your prospect's likes and dislikes. Your products and services may work for everyone, so to speak, but you must verbally relate each and every solution or recommendation you make to your prospect and what he or she has said. Don't sell the product in a manner divorced from your prospective customer's desires. You'll surely lose trust and the sale by doing that. By referring to your prospect's likes and dislikes, you maintain the trust by making it clear and explicit that you were *listening*.

Second, don't communicate your recommendations as loosely tied talking points that scatter the thoughts and lead your prospect awry. Your prospect should recognize your recommendations as a single and straightforward signal directing him or her to the best product or service. Your solution should flow smoothly like an ancient, faithful waterfall. Here's an example:

---

### EXAMPLE: MAPPING A SOLUTION

"Mr. Phillips, you mentioned to me that several months ago you called your rep for news on a new line of children's football uniforms, and he did not get back with you until six hours later because he was out on appointments. That's an understandable wait, but I understand the need for a quick answer. You won't have that wait with us. What I will do to ensure that you do not experience that problem with us is provide you with an additional service representative, so there will be two people assigned to serve you and your team. If one of them has a plate full of appointments, the other will be available to serve you when you call. We know your time is valuable."

Here is another example:

---

EXAMPLE: MAPPING A SOLUTION

You've explained to me, Mr. Walker, that you need a fast ship that will give you smooth passage and attract the right kind of attention to you. As you said, you don't want your neighbors on the gulf staring at your boat because it bounces funny on the water. You want them envying your awesome boat! I've got several vessels that meet your description, two of which are designed to minimize sea-sickness, but let's go over each in turn, their pluses and minus, so we can be sure you're buying the right boat for you and your family.

---

## PRACTICE YOUR SWING BEFORE YOU STEP UP TO THE PLATE

Here is the third thing to keep in mind when mapping solutions: *Practice*. In the previous chapter I explained how to develop your purposeful questions through practice. We need to approach mapping customer solutions with the same idea. If we are using the information we obtained from our questions, this process should be pretty simple. The tough part is developing and practicing your solution map so you express it comfortably and smoothly when talking to the prospective customer. When we are prepared we are more confident, and when we are confident our prospects will assume we are competent—unless we prove them otherwise.

> Add mapping solutions to your practice sessions. Keep it there, even if you think you've memorized the map.

Imagine you work for an exhibit company that offers products for trade show booths. You're speaking with the representative of a large company that does a few high-end trade shows a year. The following four statements are answers this prospect has provided to a few of your purposeful questions:

1. "Your exhibit company is not the least expensive in the industry."
2. "Our shipping costs are too high."
3. "We are not getting the right people in our booth."
4. "No, my current rep does not discuss proactive ideas to increase our results; he calls me a few times a year—right before each show."

Here is a solutions map you might use in response to these answers:

"Ms. Karenina, you're right: like you in your industry, we are not the least expensive. We have found through years of experience that the main goal of our customers is not to buy cheap; it is to increase profits. So that is what we focus on. We can look at your current exhibit and compare it to a more modern design, which, due to its lighter material, would decrease your overhead expense of shipping up to 40% depending on the weight of your current exhibit. We started using this lighter material about two years ago* for this exact reason. We also know that there are several companies out there that use similar materials and can build similar looking exhibits. The reason our clients choose our company relates to what you shared with me about your current struggles with not getting the right people in your booths and the lack of strategic planning by your rep: we conduct quarterly planning sessions with our key clients to 1) make sure we are proactively implementing the newest and most effective pre-show and post-show selling activities and 2) ensure the graphics of your display are achieving your desired results."

> The answers you receive to purposeful questions should mark the main points on your map of solutions.

*I mention this time period on the chance that the prospective customer is wondering why his current rep hasn't offered this more cost-effective material at anytime in the past two years.

### PLAN AND PRACTICE FOR THE UNFORESEEABLE

I want to be very clear: I am not saying that a sales professional should have a canned speech. What I'm saying is that we should practice mapping solutions based on the questions we ask so we are confident and smooth when recommending a solution. The solution will then be true to the client's likes and dislikes. Why? Because all of the recommended solutions are based on the prospect's answers.

As practicing the mapping of solutions requires you to consider not only your questions, but also your prospective client's possible answers, you would do well to brainstorm all the conceivable answers that could be given to your questions. Get together with others and put your heads together. Think about answers you've heard on the job: the common answers you can reasonably expect and the rare, out-of-the-blue answers that would totally take you by surprise.

> Every recommended solution should be based on the prospect's answers to purposeful questions!

Practice mapping solutions to all of these answers. Mix up their order. Use shuffled flashcards. At the end of the day, be able to provide a smooth, flowing, and singular response to any and every combination of answers your prospect might throw at you. You can't just practice for a single kind of play. You have to be ready for anything, from a blitz to a bomb to a quarterback sneak.

Remember: regular practice for sales professionals is just as essential as practice is for professional athletes. Don't let mapping solutions fall out of your practice program just because you've become good at it. Jim Collins said it best: "The greatest enemy of great is good."

### YOU CAN'T HIT A HOMERUN WITHOUT A BAT

In many "old school" selling skills trainings we were taught to explain the features of a product first and then show the benefits the product provides to the prospect. This order of explanation makes sense from the sales professional's and manufacture's points of view, but from the prospect's prospective, it is backwards. Prospective customers come to you in need of a benefit, not foremost a feature.

For example, a customer goes to hardware store to buy a drill. What need really sent the customer to the store? What is ultimately needed? The drill? No, the drill is a means to an end. The drill is a tool that meets the customer's need. The real need is a hole. The customer comes to Home Depot or Lowes in need of something that makes a hole. The product here is the drill, the feature is the ability to drill a hole and the result is the benefit (the hole).

Instead of starting your solution mapping from the feature, begin with the desired benefit. Find out from your prospect his or her fundamental needs, what is liked and disliked, and then go from there. If you're that sales professional at a hardware store, you'll get to the drill soon enough, so don't rush the process. You'll help the prospect find the best drill with the right features by finding out first what kind and size of hole the customer needs to make.

Start with what your prospect knows: the benefit they need.

You want to start with the benefit and not the feature because the benefit is what the prospects have in mind and what motivates them to come to you. They most likely don't know your line of products, so you don't begin with them. You begin with what the prospect has in mind – the benefit – and transition from the benefit they seek to the products you sell, from what they already know to what they don't yet know but can learn from you.

## ARE YOU A BENEFIT TO YOUR PROSPECTS?

Mapping solutions is more than just haphazardly giving features and benefits like a part-time sales clerk at the mall kiosk selling hair extensions or luscious smelling lotions. We must translate what prospective customers tell us they like and dislike into real desired benefits and then show how the features of our company or product can provide those benefits.

One of those benefits better be *you*, the sales professional. Remember this image: you are interviewing for the job, not trying to persuade someone into buying something they don't need or want.

## INFLUENCE: 33% - THE GOOD, THE BAD AND THE UGLY

During mapping solutions, you should also discuss any weakness your product or service may have and whatever the prospective client or customer may view as a negative. I repeat: by being the person to point out the perceived negatives, you show honesty, avoid having to overcome customer objections, and at the same time, help prospects make informed decisions that are right for them. You show likeability, earn their trust, and become an influence. Best of all, you *close the sale.*

### BUYING ISN'T A BLACK AND WHITE DECISION

In 2001 I was the Regional Director of Indirect Sales for Sprint. Our focus that year was to increase our local distribution from less than 3% of our distribution to over 33% of our distribution. This was a lofty goal, but the regional president at the time was no stranger to achieving lofty goals. My job was to travel the Southeast and Southwest parts of the country to help add new local retailers and to get the current local retailers to sell more.

> Always be the one to bring up possible objections. Don't ignore them and don't overcome them. Consider them!

One of the perceived weaknesses of our product was that, as a company, we were the only retailer that sold our phones with the traditional retail model. Retailers would buy products from us for wholesale and sell them retail, making a small commission right at the point of the sale but for about half that of our competitors. Our competitors did not use the traditional retail model; the retailer and the customer paid the same price for a phone, but the competition's salespeople made higher commissions than we paid, though much later.

Now I grew up as a son of a small business owner (and am now one myself), so I understood that pain of poor cash flow. I was able to relate to the retailers as a person who understood their business model and, more importantly, I was able to help them look at the pros and cons of our system and help them make the best decision for them. I taught (influenced) them that by selling our product, they instantly had better cash flow, as opposed to the competition that paid out at a much later date.

Yes, a smaller commission seemed at first to be a real negative, but I helped my prospects see that the instant cash flow more than made up for the size of the commission. Because I brought up the negative, I was positioned to be an influence. What I said in response to the negative therefore had merit.

I live by a really simple rule in sales: we make a pay check when we make a sale, but we make a living when we make a customer ecstatic, when we help customers make the best decisions for themselves in the long run.

## MOVING TO THE NEXT STEP OF INFLUENCE

Mapping solutions is truly where we bring the sales call together to prepare for the close. Although we are closing during the entire sales call, from creating likeability to earning trust to becoming the influencer, mapping solutions is where a sales person gets his first real grade.

If the prospective customer says, "Great, thanks, we will call you," you might have missed something, and you'd best find out what that was. If the prospective client gives you a check, then shut up and leave. Politely and appreciatively, of course.

Most of us, however, will find that we must go to the next step of influence: consideration.     In old school selling they called it overcoming objections, but I believe you cannot win a sale by overcoming someone; rather you must help them make the best decision.

## CHAPTER FIVE HIGHLIGHTS

- Trust can take weeks and months to gain, but can be lost in seconds.

- Always offer solutions based explicitly on the answers your customer gave to your purposeful questions.

- Be open and honest about any weaknesses.

- No one likes to be sold, but everyone likes to buy things. The difference is in how and when we map solutions.

# 6

# INFLUENCE:
# CONSIDERATION

Con·sid·er·a·tion (kən-,si-də'rā-shən) n. 1. *Careful deliberation*

It makes no sense to throw prospects to the tiled floor in an effort to influence them, and yet the old school method of overcoming objections often results in prospects feeling as if they'd been tackled on a hard surface. Trying to overcome the prospect's objections tends to leave the prospect feeling *personally* overcome.

In my playbook, the very word *overcome* is a problem.

It can simply mean surmounting some difficulty, but it can also mean *battling* or *conquering*. You can see this difference of meaning when I say that a soldier can overcome his fears or overcome his enemies. If *overcoming* had only the former definition and not the latter, I wouldn't take issue with its use.

> "Fall down seven times. Stand up eight."
>
> - Japanese Proverb

Unfortunately, too often in practice, and sometimes in intent, salespeople have the latter in mind when they face off against the prospect's objections. Envisioning them as an enemy on the field of battle, they draw the sword, raise the banner, and charge the objections without fear of consequence. These salespeople may win the debate, but, more-often-than-not, they lose the sale. The prospects feel defeated, irked or frustrated, but definitely not influenced. And the salespeople find no victory in their prospect's retreat.

Instead of teaching salespeople to overcome objections, I instruct would-be sales professionals to help the prospect *consider* all options. Think about it: when was the last time you made a decision after considering the pros and cons of that decision? Unless you're the impulsive type, you most likely you do it all the time. If a sales professional can show prospects that they want to help them make the best decision by looking at all the pros and cons together, then the sales professional has become an influencer who has the prospect's best interests in mind.

Remember my advice earlier: treat the prospect as you would your mom. You wouldn't try to overcome or do battle with your mom in a disagreement over a product. You would try to help her make the best choice for her. Do the same for your prospective customers, even if it means them not buying from you.

## CONSIDERATION: 33% - RELAX

Relax. Seriously. To be effective at consideration, the very first thing you must do is *relax*.

If you are doing what you should be doing, the possible negatives of your product or service will be front and center in your discussion. Relax. They should be. When prospective clients share with us reasons they feel they should not buy our product or service, they are doing what any person would do when making a decision. They are considering.

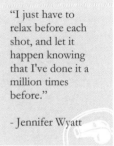

"I just have to relax before each shot, and let it happen knowing that I've done it a million times before."

- Jennifer Wyatt

### WHY YOU ARE THERE?

You are not there to stop them from considering by means of redirection or other distractions; you are there to help them through the consideration process. They can't make the best decisions without considering the pros and cons. Relax. Every product and service ever sold has pros and cons.

What if the prospect brings up the negatives? Don't panic! Again, take a deep breath and *relax*. In most cases objections are *good*. They mean that prospects are putting some *thought* into their decisions. If they're thinking, they're not blowing you off. People don't go to sales professionals to raise objections for the sake of raising objections. They go to blog com-boxes for that.

Raising negatives isn't overcoming objections, not if you are helping prospects to consider their options. The real objection, the one you don't want to hear, is, "Thanks for your time or information; we will call you." But even if you do hear something to this effect, don't panic. Ask the prospect if there is something you haven't addressed. Give the impression (or say flat out) that you want the prospect to raise concerns about the product. You overcome these real objections, these thoughtless disregards of what you have to offer, by helping your prospects, especially those who feel uncomfortable about a purchase, to make the best decision for them.

## RELAX BY RAISING THE OBJECTIONS

One way to relax is to be the one who *brings up* the objections. By doing so you steer the conversation towards consideration, show true concern and honesty about your project, and avoid waiting anxiously for the prospect to raise objections, wondering how you will respond to them. By raising them yourself, you can frame them in a way that fits nicely into a casual but forthright consideration of the product's pros and cons.

Relax and ask questions in a way that allows your prospect to relax as well.

When you raise possible objections, make sure you are the one who actually raises them. Some salespeople think that they have raised objections when they ask the prospect to think of objections. They have done nothing of the sort.

Think about the infamous car salesperson asking, "If I can do X, would you buy the car today?" Is this question raising objections? No! The car salesperson is asking the prospects to raise them, and not so he or she can help them carefully consider their choices. The intent of these types of questions is not the intent you should have. Nor is the tone of the questions the tone you want to express. You don't want to put the prospect on the spot. You want to help them consider the pluses and minuses and make the right decision for them.

## RAISE SPECIFIC CONCERNS, NOT VAGUE ONES

When I say raise "objections" yourself, I mean raise them specifically, in concrete detail. You know the possible downside of your product or service, or at least you should. If you don't yet know the benefits your prospect seeks and what he or she is currently experiencing, if you don't know how your offerings compare and contrast with those of the competition, then you have no business being in this state of the sales process yet. You can't help prospects consider without knowing what they need to consider. So, if your service has unique compatibility issues or takes more technical know-how, raise these possible concerns.

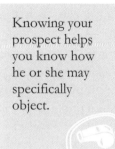

Knowing your prospect helps you know how he or she may specifically object.

Get them out in the open and in plain sight. Go over them with the prospect. Help your prospects know everything they need to know about the product so they are not nervously wondering if you're hiding some downside they'll discover later to their detriment. By being the one to raise the concerns, you help not only yourself to relax, but you help your prospect to relax as well!

## KEEP YOUR EYE ON THE BALL

Here's an example of the sales professional raising concerns: "Ms. Johnson, I know we discussed a lot of things today, and it might be beneficial if we look at the pros and cons of buying from my organization. The first thing I think we need to look at is the upfront cost you or your organization will incur by going with us. These are…"

Notice what you would be doing here: First, you are framing the consideration process within the larger sales process. This helps the prospect keep in mind everything you've said as you move into considering the pros and cons. Second, you are acknowledging, sincerely and confidently, that, yes, your product or service has perceived drawbacks. You come across as serious and professional about yourself, your prospect, your product or service, and the consideration process. You come across as a likeable and confident professional who knows what he or she is doing and wants what's best for the prospects. That image, I challenge you, should be the stereotype of the sales professional.

## WATCH YOUR PROSPECT DEFEND YOUR PRODUCT

When you bring up possible objections to your product or service, you will be surprised at how many times the prospective customer will be the one to start to find the pros to offset the cons! You bring up initial start-up fees; your prospect brings up long-term financial benefit. You raise the potential difficulty the client's team may have learning a new system; your prospect counters that the team could use something new and exciting to boost their anticipation for new projects.

Raising concerns scares many salespeople. They feel that perhaps they are helping the prospect find the negatives or objections that may not even be an issue until the prospect hears and dwells upon them. What if the sales professional raises a deal-breaking objection that hadn't popped in the prospect's mind? Wouldn't the sales professional be shooting himself in the foot?

> In professional sales, it can pay to be the bearer of bad news.

This fear is similar to what I hear from some salespeople who tell me they don't ask what a prospective customer likes about their current vendor because they don't want the prospect to think of all of the good things about their competition.

Here is a news flash: they *are* thinking about it whether or not you bring it up. Imagining otherwise is like a student hoping that the teacher won't check to see that the homework has been completed. Here's the thing: if *you* don't bring it up, *you* won't be around to be a part of the decision and remove some of those concerns. You will be given the "I'll think about it" blow off while your lost prospect thinks about the objections you didn't want to bring up.

## WHAT SHOULD ACTUALLY WORRY YOU

In sales and customer service, it not what the prospect tells you that should worry you; it is what they are not telling you. If the prospective customer is conversing with you and showing interest about your product, then you're on the right path. It's the prospect who brushes you off or eludes you or seems agitated and impatient in your company that should be giving you red flags. The ones actually talking with you, especially at this stage of consideration, are waving green flags. Go! Keep moving. And relax!

In business and consumer sales, there is a short-term inconvenience like cost, learning curve and implementation. Most prospective customers know this. You don't need to hide or evade these inconveniences. Raise them and put them – or allow your prospect to put them – in perspective and context. For example, remind your prospective client of the age-old truth that the worst thing a business can do is make a long-term decision based on a short term inconvenience.

# CONSIDERATION: 33% - POSITIONING

You can identify whether you are considering with the prospective customers or if you are overcoming their objections by assessing your position. Your position is where you are sitting in this discussion, not physically, but metaphorically. Are you on the same side of the table helping to seek solutions by looking at all of the pros and cons or are you on the other side of the desk trying to defend your position?

"Don't organize in the spirit of antagonism; that should be beneath your consideration."

- Mark Hanna

When you are on the other side of the desk, you find yourself making statements such as, "But you said you did not like X" or "Did you not say you wanted to change Y?" When you act as though you're sitting across a desk defending your position, you put your prospective customer in the same defensive position. Soon enough your prospect is defending his or her current position. You start to lose ground and eventually lose the sale. The prospect feels overcome and overwhelmed. You lose business.

## WHEN NOT TO SELL

Instead, if during the consideration you realize that the customer will not benefit from your product or service, acknowledge that fact and move on. Would you want your mother to buy something that did not benefit her? Of course not! Remember: treat your prospects like you would your mother. Your job is not to sell by any means necessary; it is to sell the products or services that are right for your prospects.

> Yes, there are times when not to sell. But don't let these go to waste.

It may be hard to believe, but your product isn't always the right fit. If you acknowledge that, rather than try to force feed your product, you will gain more sales in the long run. The prospects will remember you when someone they meet *is* a good fit. They will recommend you because of your honesty. I know this from experience. Telling your prospects that your product isn't a fit for them is a short-term inconvenience for you as a sales professional, but it pays off in the long-term with additional business and a solid reputation for good sales professionalism.

## YOU BETTER HAVE FOLLOWED THE STEPS

A final remark about position: you may find yourself sitting across the table, metaphorically speaking, because you didn't discover your prospective customer's likes and dislikes or build trust during the *Trust* and *Mapping Solutions* stages. If this is the case, all may not be lost, but you have an uphill battle with consideration. And, as I explained, being in a battle is not what you want to be doing during the consideration stage. It's counter-productive and risks not only the loss of the sale, but also the loss of future business. You cannot fly through the early stages and expect to succeed at consideration anymore than a math student cannot ace algebra having a weak, slippery grasp of multiplication and division.

Fortunately, if you're reading this book, you're not (I hope) in the middle of the consideration process, so you can make sure that, in the future, you take sufficient time building likeability, trust and influence before you embark on mapping solutions and considering with the prospect. Doing the early steps correctly helps put you in the right position for consideration.

## CONSIDERATION: 33% - BE PART OF THE DECISION

The chief goal of the consideration part of a sales call is to remove obstacles by weighing the pros and cons. Another goal is to remove any "fake objections" from consideration. You can't really remove a "fake objection," so instead of trying to overcome an obstacle that may be a smoke screen, it is better to have the prospect explain what he or she is presenting as an objection. You can do this by asking the

Don't hesitate to clear the air if you see a smoke screen.

question, "That is an interesting point, why do you feel that way?" If it is not a real obstacle or is just a smoke screen, the prospect will struggle with the answer. If it is a smoke screen, the key is not to push the prospective customer in the corner; rather, try and identify why the prospect is giving you the smoke screen excuse. If you can find out the why, then you will be in the position to resolve the real issue *together*.

## FOLLOW THROUGH ON YOUR SWING

There are only two logical steps after consideration; asking for the sale or moving on to the next prospective customer.   I have found that too many salespeople just leave the meeting without closing, even if the answer is "No."   Salespeople I meet tell me that they don't ask because they feel that as long as the prospect did not say, "No," there still may be a chance, however slim, that the prospect will say, "Yes," even despite body language and statements indicating a resounding "No."

The excuse reminds me of the scene in the movie *Dumb and Dumber* in which Jim Carey asks the girl about the chances of a girl like her going out with a guy like him, she says one in a million, and he idiotically proclaims, "So you're saying there's a chance!"

The scene is funny in the movie, but it's just sad in sales.  Know your value so the prospect will know it too.  Don't be timid.  If the product or service is right for the prospect, then ask for the sale.  Just as you can't get a job without asking for it after the interview, you can't get business without asking for it at the end of the sales call.

## PLAY 110% EACH INNING TO THE END OF THE SALE

You should really be implicitly asking for the sale throughout the sales call.  If you have established all three positions with the prospective customer and *considered* the decision with the customer—you have the right to ask for the business.

Close the sale with a concrete plan of action for the next step!

When asking for the sale, every sales professional needs a closing question, and, in some cases, a few different closing questions. If you sell B to B (business-to-business), an option might be; "So do you want to start shipments this Monday or next Monday?" The question moves you forward with something concrete and practical.  It's good to walk away with a "Yes," but it's much better and smarter to walk away with that "Yes" and a tangible game plan for what comes next.

Closing a sale is straightforward, and like most things in sales, it is a simple concept, but not necessarily easy to do. We don't want to be pushy, yet at the same time we need to ask for the business. When asking for the business, just as throughout the rest of the sales process, it is important to be *you*. In my sales trainings, I discuss the principles and *intent* of our actions, but the words and actions have to be *your* words and actions. So give this some thought and don't leave it to chance.

## RECAP

Sometimes you can close a sale immediately after mapping solutions, but most likely you'll need to help your prospects through the consideration process before they'll write and hand you a check.

Before you consider the pros and cons of the prospect's decision, take a deep breath, remember your purpose, and relax. If the product or service isn't right for your prospect, don't worry about it. Recommend that the prospect consider not buying from you, but ask the prospect to send you business if he or she comes upon someone who could use your product or service.

When you lead the prospect through considering the decision, position yourself on the same side of the table as the prospect, so to speak. You're not an adversary. You're not an enemy. You're not an opponent. You are a guide, an influencer, a sales professional!

Finally, be part of the decision. Ask for the business if the prospect expresses an interest or what you have is a good fit. Follow through on your swing and close the sale.

## CHAPTER SIX HIGHLIGHTS

- You can win the battle and lose the sale.

- Relax!

- Be on the same side of the table as your prospect.

- Treat prospects as you would family (that you like).

- Long-term benefits demand short-term costs.

- Be a part of the decision.

# 7

# CREATING YOUR SALES PLAN

plan (plăn) n. 1. *A scheme, program, or method worked out beforehand for the accomplishment of an objective*

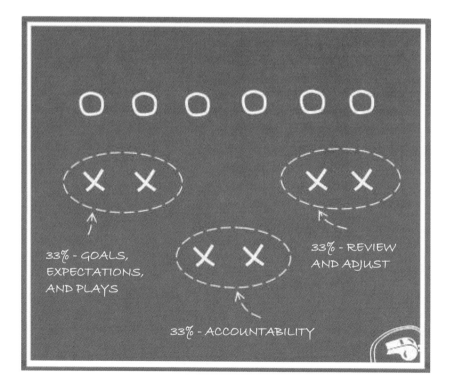

Every football team has a game plan, every army has a battle plan, and every sales professional needs a sales plan.

Without a game plan, even a talented football team won't be prepared for the plays of an opposing team. Any coach worth his coach's cap knows that it takes more to win than getting the ball and running toward the end zone. The players have to know their roles, what they should expect from one another, how they're going to advance with each and every play of the game, and anything and everything the opposition can throw at them.

"Our goals can only be reached through a vehicle of a plan, in which we must fervently believe, and upon which we must vigorously act."

- Pablo Picasso

The coach has to plan for every contingency and help set in place a planned organizational structure designed for maximum success. He has to keep the players engaged in fulfilling the game plan.

Team owners know the importance of game plans as well. That's why they're justified in firing the coach when the team performs poorly. Even a great team will be a losing team without an effective game plan.

Without a battle plan, even the best of soldiers will find themselves in disadvantageous situations. There's a horrific scene in the miniseries *Band of Brothers* in which the men of Easy Company, an elite force if there ever was one, find themselves fatally exposed to enemy fire because their temporary, inexperienced commanding officer fails to give them a battle plan.

Once they're provided a course of action that allows the unit to attack as a unified force, they are able to reposition themselves and escape the unorganized chaos and pulverization that would have utterly destroyed them. There are also some daring heroics done to make sure all the soldiers know the plan and are on the same page.

As sales professionals, we tend to think that we don't need to plan; we just need to get out there and *do it*. Perhaps we think this way because when our unplanned *doing* fails we don't have thousands of fans upset with us and we haven't put our very lives at risk. Sure, we might say, the athlete and the soldier need a plan, obviously, but we're different.

Well, we are different, obviously, but our being different is no excuse for not having a plan. We don't need a football game plan, per se, and clearly we don't need a battle plan, but we do need a *sales* plan.

### AN IDEA IS NOT A PLAN

Why do we sales professionals need a sales plan? Because without a plan, we don't really know what it is we're doing when we go out there and do it. We don't have a clear sense of where we are, where we want to go, and what we need to do, step-by-step, to get there.

We also don't really know where we're going because we don't have a way to assess and analyze what we're doing. We just do it and hope for the best. Or we think we have a plan when we really don't. Sometimes this works temporarily, but then we find ourselves chasing shadows or wandering aimlessly.

> "It takes as much energy to wish as it does to plan."
>
> - Eleanor Roosevelt

Sales professionals tell me all the time that they have a plan: one that is in their head. That is not a plan. That is a thought. I once heard someone say the difference between a funny person and a comedian is that a comedian writes down his or her thoughts. Comedians plan their comedy. Funny people just do it. I don't have to tell you which one gets paid for being funny.

Getting it down on paper or a word processor is what makes it a plan and not merely a thought. Writing down your plan allows you to actually plan and build upon your plan. You could, conceivably, formulate a plan in your head without writing it down, but then you forget parts and the plan unravels.

As you'll see below, creating a plan has a number of steps, and once it's completed you'll want to go back to it again and again. You'll need to be able to see it, analyze it, and review it, so *write it down*.

### BECOMING MORE THAN A TOP PERFORMER

I was fortunate enough early in my sales career that one of my leaders pulled me aside and told me that if I wanted to take my sales to the next level (I happened already to be a top performer), I needed to put together a sales plan. Like most successful sales professionals, I didn't think I needed one, but I respected this leader and tried it. I have never looked back.

That was in the early 90's, and since then I have helped hundreds of sales professionals develop their sales plans. I have seen these plans change and develop over the last twenty years and have happily watched them take low, medium and high performers to the very top of their organizations.

## CREATING A SALES PLAN: 33% - GOALS, EXPECTATIONS AND PLAYS

> Plan your work for today and every day, then work your plan.
>
> - Margaret Thatcher

What should your sales plan tell you?

It should tell you where you are and where you want to be (i.e. your goals). Most importantly, it should indicate how you are going to get there.

Again, a vague idea is not a plan. You could probably succeed at driving from the East Coast to the West Coast without any maps or signs if you drove more or less in a westerly direction, but without a driving plan, there's no way you'll make a trip from West Almond, New York to Temecula, California, let alone make good time and drive with the minimum amount of miles.

## WHAT A GOOD SALES PLAN TELLS YOU

A plan for a cross-country drive tells you where you are, where you're going, and how you are going to get there. It can help you see the sights you want to see and travel with the least amount of expense. These days it can also help you avoid congestion or areas of heavy construction.

A sales plan likewise tells you where you are, where you are going, and the steps you need to take to be prepared to close the sales and become a top performer. Like a plan for a cross-country trip, the sales plan gives you general directions and specific instructions.

## TO THE TOP AND BEYOND

Think of your sales plan as a map for getting to that top spot in your sales profession. Really picture it as such. I say this again and again to people, and will keep saying it until I lose my voice: knowledge is not power; what you *do* with your knowledge is what gives you power. Most sales professionals have an idea of what to do (they see it, heard about it, etc.), but very few have a plan to actually do it. Unless you put your knowledge into a plan, and put that plan into action, your knowledge does not become power and remains useless—"less used" or not used at all.

> "You were born to win, but to be a winner, you must plan to win, prepare to win, and expect to win."
>
> - Zig Zigler

## YOUR PLAN SHOULD NEVER LOOK LIKE NEW

Success in sales is *not an accident*; it the execution of a purposeful plan. A great sales plan does not have to be pretty and stored in a colorful three-ring binder. It should be coffee-stained, wrinkled, and show signs of your constant use. It should never be shelved and forgotten like those encyclopedias people buy only to fill their book shelf and create the appearance of knowledge. It should never pass for "Like New" at a used bookstore.

## THREE COMPONENTS

The first couple of sales plans you write will be the most difficult, but I promise they get easier and more effective as you go. A sales plan should have three components:

**Component One**: **Where are you now and what are you doing now?** Include your current results (numbers) and your current activities.

When looking at your sales numbers, look at the previous quarter and also the previous year (if applicable). Let's assume we are doing a quarterly business plan for the $1^{st}$ quarter.

First, get your January through March numbers from last year and numbers from the most recent quarter. Depending on your industry you may need to use your own seasonal adjustments.

If you're a rookie who's just getting started, you obviously won't have real numbers to jot down. For now, you can use industry averages or what you think are reasonable numbers, but once you have some experience, revise your plan to include an accurate assessment of where you currently are.

> Determine where you are and plan where you're going.

Second, lay out all of your selling activities; these include current and new clients, prospecting activities (including networking groups and referrals), whatever is in your pipeline, what upcoming appointments and events you have, and so forth. Include whatever you are doing to build your business right this minute.

Basically, you want to put down all relevant information that indicates where you are as a sales professional. Again, if you are just getting started in the sales profession, put down what you will be doing in the next few days and weeks.

**Component Two:** Where do you want to go? For this component, use two sets of goals: long-term annual goals and short-term quarterly goals.

Annual goals are usually results based, whereas quarterly goals are going to be both activity-based and results-based. Here is a sample of some sales goals:

EXAMPLES: ANNUAL GOALS

✓ I want to do one million dollars in sales this year.
✓ I want to make $270,000 in commissions.
✓ I want to close these 20 key companies by year-end.
✓ I want to have over 150 prospects in my funnel.
✓ I want to be promoted by December 31st.

EXAMPLES: QUARTERLY GOALS

✓ Sell $300,000 in first quarter; a 25% increase year over year.
✓ Set appointments with these 10 key companies (should be 10 of the 20 of your annual goal).
✓ Stick to my prospecting plan and add 40 new qualified prospects to my funnel.
✓ Proactively gain 20 new referrals from my current customer.

Notice that "I want to make $270,000 in commissions" indicates a result of what you plan to put into practice. It's a results-based goal. "Stick to my prospecting plan and add 40 new qualified prospects to my funnel" indicates both an activity and a result.

**Component Three:  How are you going to get there?**  This is one of the most important parts of your sales plan and where the magic really happens.   It's also the component that most needs your commitment.

To get started with this component of your sales plan, think of two things:

1. Who are you going to contact?
2. How are you going to contact them?

**Who:** Identify your target market. Write it down.  I like to have three different markets (or funnels) so that my sales profession has enough legs to stand on—like a three-legged stool.  With only one or two markets in my plan, I risk toppling over like an unsupported stool.

**How**: Now that you've identified your markets, compose prospect lists that indicate *how you will contact prospects.*

**Prospect List 1:** Vertical market.  Identify key prospects to contact. Then identify two events this quarter where you can meet these prospects. Finally, create a plan of action for meeting each one.

> Plan *who* you are going to contact and *how* you are going to contact them.

I worked with a successful sales professional named Peggy who wanted to focus on fire departments.  First, she identified 12 of the local fire departments that she wanted to target.  Then she put together a plan to set appointments with the chief of each fire department.

Peggy indentified the *who* and planned the *how*. She then went and conducted a presentation with each fire station house during one of their many team dinners. This, of course, required a little research about the fire stations, their personnel, and their plans and upcoming events.

Within 90 days Peggy had achieved her goal and conducted sales presentations with all 12 fire departments. She even found that once she got in the first one, each department helped her to get into the next one. Needless to say she ended up generating business from every single fire house.

You can see the template of her sales plan in how she identified the market (fire departments), identified the prospects (the twelve chiefs), and identified events at which to give sales presentations (team dinners). Peggy wrote the plan down, executed her plan over a period of three months (one quarter), and achieved her goals because she planned exactly how she wanted to reach them and how she would reach them based on her research.

Plan your prospecting proactively!

If you have trouble thinking of prospects, try looking at the local businesses in your area that would benefit from your product or service. Search the Internet, scan industry magazines, attend trade shows, identify target markets, and network. (See Chapter 9 for more ways to build a prospect pipeline).

**Prospect List 2:** Current Customer referrals. Too many times in sales we twiddle our thumbs and wait for one of our clients to recommend us to someone unprompted. We want to know we are doing a good job and that of course each of our clients will *eventually* recommend us, right? We desire that unasked for affirmation, and yet we may or may not get it while we just assume the ball is in their court.

Yeah, that extra affirmation boosts our ego, but we're not in this business to boost our egos. We're in it to boost our sales. Instead of waiting for our customers and clients to work for us unprompted, we need to work at staying foremost in their thoughts so that they'll automatically recommend us when the occasion presents itself.

As the saying goes, be proactive rather than reactive. Stay in contact with your customers and clients. Send them a card or pick up the phone to touch base. Don't let yourself be forgotten.

Go even further. Ask customers and clients if they know anyone you can help. There's no shame in this, no wound to one's pride. Ask away!

Our customers and clients have busy lives to live; they're not always thinking about us and about getting us future business. It's our job to get us business, not theirs. Nevertheless, you will be surprised at how receptive they are to your call and how eager they are to help.

So pick ten of your current customers and ask each of them to give you two referrals, two people to whom you may be of service and to whom you can introduce yourself. If only five of your customers give you two referrals, that is still ten new quality prospects to add to your pipeline.

**Before executing your plan, scrimmage it.**

I had a sales professional who I was working with in 2009 who had a great relationship with her clients. She made a list of three customers to call each week and ask for referrals. She created a script that we worked on together and we did several scrimmages prior to her making the calls (scripts are essential, but so is being sincere and natural). In just three weeks she had gotten two new qualified referrals, and one of those referrals became a very, very large sale.

Again, this is not rocket science—*it is simply having and executing a plan.* You can't just say to yourself that you'll get to finding referrals one of these days. That's just procrastinating and you'll quickly discover that "one of these days" never arrives. Only you can make that day arrive, so make a plan and execute it.

And make writing and executing your plan a permanent part of your profession. Making the plan isn't a one-time deal that sets you up for life. Your professional life has to be about following the sales plan.

## THE BASICS MAKE GREAT PLAYS

Include in the third component of your plan the expectations you have for yourself—the basic tasks that need to be done. Write these down as reminders because it is so easy to get caught up in email, returning non-revenue generating phone calls, getting stuck by the water cooler gossiping, etc. These expectations and activities will fluctuate and need to be personalized depending on your industry, but here are some examples.

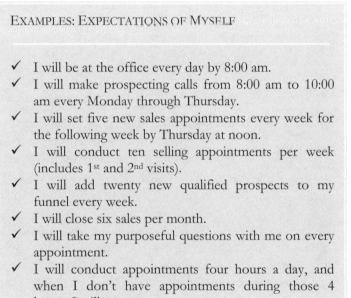

### EXAMPLES: EXPECTATIONS OF MYSELF

- ✓ I will be at the office every day by 8:00 am.
- ✓ I will make prospecting calls from 8:00 am to 10:00 am every Monday through Thursday.
- ✓ I will set five new sales appointments every week for the following week by Thursday at noon.
- ✓ I will conduct ten selling appointments per week (includes 1st and 2nd visits).
- ✓ I will add twenty new qualified prospects to my funnel every week.
- ✓ I will close six sales per month.
- ✓ I will take my purposeful questions with me on every appointment.
- ✓ I will conduct appointments four hours a day, and when I don't have appointments during those 4 hours, I will prospect.

These are all basic tasks and expectations that you should be able to complete without any excuses. Writing them down and reviewing them helps keep you on task and helps keep you on the course you have planned. Letting these fall by the wayside risks redirecting you away from your stated goals.

# CREATING A SALES PLAN: 33%- ACCOUNTABILITY

*Share your plan!* In order to make sure you fully execute your plan, ask for help to hold yourself accountable.  As a sales leader I mandated that all of my sales professionals create a sales plan and then present them to the entire team, including to their manager and their manager's manager.

I found that when we publically say we are going to do something, we are more likely to do it. If we are the only ones who know our plan, then we are less likely to do it.  No one else is holding us accountable to it, so it's easy to hold ourselves to a lower standard.

## PUT YOUR BOSS AND PEERS TO WORK

> Why did I outperform my peers? Because I had a plan and I executed it.

If your boss does not require a plan of action, then volunteer one to him or her.  Early in my career, I had a boss who did not require us to have sales plans, but since my previous mentor and leader did, I already had the practice and discipline in place.  So every quarter I would go to my boss and say here is my 90-day plan.

Not only did my boss appreciate this information, some of my peers eventually wanted to know why I was always outperforming them.  I showed them the plan I had showed my boss, and pretty soon they were writing and executing sales plans as well.

## ACCOUNTABILITY: THE MORE THE BETTER

It's a fact of life that we don't hold ourselves as accountable as others hold us when we have asked them to.  Even sales professionals with the most self-discipline succeed more when they ask others to hold their feet to the fire.  I'd wager your boss wouldn't turn down the opportunity to do so, but if he or she isn't interested or hasn't the time, then solicit the aid of your colleagues and peers.

Sharing your sales plan also benefits you by having your plan critiqued by others. As I note in the next section, even the best of plans needs review and adjustment. You can get constructive feedback right away by sharing your plan. You can also share ideas and learn from your fellow sales professionals.

## CREATING A SALES PLAN: 33% - REVIEW AND ADJUST QUARTERLY

Your plan should be reviewed and adjusted quarterly, by you if not by your peers and manager. You will find that some things worked great and others did not work so well. Your plan isn't meant to be written in stone. You didn't receive it from the mountain top. It wasn't composed centuries ago. It's a recent and very living document, one in need of your revision as you put it into practice and see how well (or poorly) it works.

It's a historical fact that what looks good on paper doesn't always play well in the real world. You have to consider the real world when reviewing your plan, just as a map-maker has to consider geographical developments when revising a map.

### DON'T LET YOUR PLAN HOLD YOU BACK

If you don't review and adjust your sales plan, it can become a crutch or an anchor that keeps you stuck in mediocrity, doing the same thing day in and day out regardless of efficiency and success. The sales plan is meant to propel you forward, not hold you back. If it's not working, don't hesitate to fiddle with it.

> "I have never worked a day in my life without selling. If I believe in something, I sell it, and I sell it hard."
>
> - Estée Lauder

And don't be afraid to try new things. Get best practices from your peers! Suppose you learn of some new sales practices that have worked really well for others. Want to see if they work for you? Well, put them in your plan and find out. With new practices in your plan and on paper, rather than just in your head, you have something definitive to look at when assessing how well the practices worked for you.

As I said earlier, a sales plan should have coffee stains, torn pages and look like your favorite magazine. No matter if you struggle with it or find it exciting and fun; make creating, executing, and adjusting your sales plan a practice you never stop no matter what level you obtain, who your boss is or what industry you are in.

You will never see a coach take the football field without a plan no matter how long he or she has been coaching—we should take to the sales field with a plan no matter how long we've been in sales.

## CHAPTER SEVEN HIGHLIGHTS

- *Every* sales professional needs to have a plan.

- The first couple of plans will be the most difficult; eventually they will become easy and effective.

- Sales plans have three components: current numbers, goals and activities to reach them.

- Share your plan for feedback and accountability.

- Plans should be coffee stained and used; not pretty and shelved.

- Plans should be reviewed and adjusted quarterly.

# 8

# PRACTICE MAKES PROFIT

prac•tice ('prak tes) v. 1. *To exercise one's self in, for improvement, or to acquire discipline or dexterity*

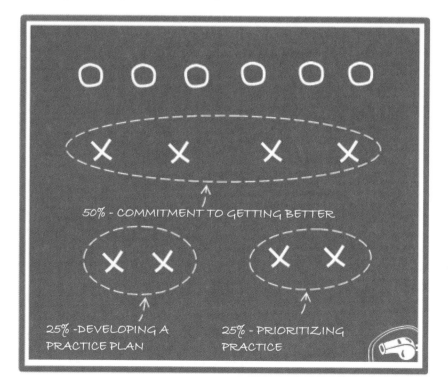

Sports teams and athletes spend 90% of their time practicing and 10% of their time playing the game. In sales, however, we spend less than 1% of the time practicing and 99% of our time playing the game. If a successful sales team requires the same elements that make up a successful sports team (like a great leader, drafting the best players, teamwork, positive mental attitudes, the execution of skills, etc.), then why are we overlooking the most important element – practice?

Think about that for a minute and ask yourself this question: "How high could your sales increase if you were to put a practice system in place?"

"Whenever an individual or a business decides that success has been attained, progress stops."

- Thomas J. Watson Jr.

The difference between an amateur and a professional is that the professional practices and gets paid very well to perform his or her skills. In the world of sales, there are salespeople (amateurs) and there are sale professionals. Both play the game, but what distinguishes the sales professional more than anything else is the practice he or she does routinely to improve his or her game. Both salespeople and sales professionals may recognize their need for much improvement, but where salespeople wallow in their mediocrity, sales professionals strive to be the best. They pursue excellence through practice.

In sales today, most companies like to talk about training or practice, but few actually translate their talk into action. Of course, we need to be realistic – we cannot practice 90% of our time and also achieve our goals. It is just not feasible. However, we can implement a regular practice schedule. With regular practice, not only can we achieve given goals, we can *overachieve* them. We can go beyond them and push ourselves to ever greater profits. By setting aside time for you to practice, you will improve your skills and your numbers – practice *will* make profits.

Before going any further, I want to make sure I am being clear. I have helped hundreds of companies over the past decade implement a practice program. These practice programs include weekly, monthly, and quarterly sessions. When I refer to practice, I mean actual *practicing*. I do not meaning training. The practice that sales professionals need should be focused on improving their selling skills. Practice is different from learning a new product and how it works. It is different than training.

## PRACTICE: 25% - DEVELOPING A PLAN

When I was an executive over the Indirect Retail Sales division of a major telecommunications company, I announced to my sales managers that we were going to initiate a team wide practice program. The practice program would focus on negotiation skills, training skills, selling skills, and role-playing. I asked my sales managers to have a 45-minute practice session every week with their sales teams as part of this new development program. I also asked groups of two to three of my sales teams to get together monthly in order to practice with each other for two hours. Then, once per quarter, my entire team would meet and practice together for eight hours.

> Practice helps make excellent what you already do well.

For the quarterly practice sessions, I asked all of my managers to work together to create the practice schedule, which would help take our entire team to the next level. Quarter to quarter, most of the topics were not changed – we regularly focused on negotiation skills, training skills, selling skills, and role-playing. Our goal was *making excellent* the same skills, thereby, taking our team to the next level.

Within two years of implementing the program, our division became number one in the nation. I attribute much of our success to the constant focus the managers and sales professionals placed on developing a practice program and executing this program daily. In other words, not only did they participate in the practice sessions, they actually implemented what they learned into their daily work lives.

As a sales professional, you can approach your leader and ask to put together a program. If you feel that the reception to your proposal will be low, then partner with a mentor or fellow sales professional, perhaps someone in a different office or a different field, and put together a practice plan—one you can implement together and incorporate into your sales plan.

## WRITING THE BASICS

How exactly you write and organize your plan is up to you, but it should be a regular and routine regiment that gives you sufficient practice in all aspects of selling and all the skills of a sales professional. Consider your weakness and work on those, but don't forget to practice those skills that you already do well.

## THINKING AHEAD

Write the plan, implement it, assess it, revise it, and be accountable to it.

It may help to plan out your practice plan for the full year. Write down all of the skills and actions you want to practice in the next 52 weeks, and then plot them into your plan. Make sure you keep coming back to the basics, but be sure to try out new things and practice higher level selling skills as well.

Don't hesitate to change your plan as you progress through it. If you feel you're spending too much time on one skill at the expense of another, assign more sessions to the latter and fewer to the former.

Keep track of the skills you're practicing, how often you practice them, and how often you use them in the game. Think short-term and long-term

It's not enough to write a plan. You have to implement it and be accountable to it. Get together with other sales professionals and put together a joint plan that has you meeting at scheduled times each week to practice and scrimmage and discuss your progress. Your practice plan should look like the sales plan I wrote about before: it should show signs of much use and revision. It should be a part of your day, and your day should be a part of it.

## WHAT DOES A PRACTICE PLAN LOOK LIKE?

Everybody's situation is different; some sales professionals sell direct to consumers, others sell direct to businesses, and yet others may sell indirectly, meaning they "influence or sell" to someone else who actually sells their product (preferably over the competitor).

Not only are the prospects different, but the environments are different as well: retail stores differ from business offices, coffee shops meetings differ from meeting in someone's home.

Lastly, the products vary as much as prospects and environments; a sales professional can be selling a tangible item like a car or house, or an intangible item like insurance or a service.

Regardless of who the prospect is or where your office is located or what you sell, there is a practice program that will work for you, but you must want one and not just say you want one. I say this because it is really easy to say, "Yeah that might work in other industries, but ours is *different,* so it won't work." Well, that is nothing but a BIG FAT excuse!

Here's a simple, yet effective practice program:

1. Call a peer and share a best practice once per week (call different peers each week). If you don't have peers, then go outside your company or even industry. *Think big.*
2. Start everyday with a song, an audio book or regular book; anything that you can listen to, watch or read that will get you ready for the day. You have the time—make it happen.
3. Have a weekly group practice session with peers (or mentors).
4. Once a quarter, spend a full day practicing, learning and working on next quarter's business plan.

5. Before sitting down to make prospecting calls, role-play or scrimmage with a co-worker to get loose.
6. Before going on a sales appointment, practice with a peer, manager or mentor.

You might find that you can only implement one or two of these ideas right away. That is fine. Any time you increase your practice, you will increase your income. In many cases, though, a sales professional can do all of these in less than three hours per week. Many sales people say they can't afford the time to practice; I say you can't afford not to practice.

Here is a scenario that will give you an idea of a weekly practice program:

**Description**: A business-to-business sales professional works in an office with several peers, but also has some peers in other offices that are far away.

**Forum**: Self and two or three other sales professionals (in person) practice specific topics (see below).

**Location**: The office; main conference room

**Time**: 8:00 am

**Frequency**: Every Monday

**Identify topics**: Telemarketing, cold calling, understanding, asking purposeful questions, consideration, etc.

**Important steps**: Have an agenda, practice for at least an hour and outline what you want to work on. Consider using one of the topics above.

**Specific Agenda**: Developing purposeful questions (30 minutes in preparation, 30 minutes in scrimmages and feedback).

Purposeful questions help us understand the prospects' goals and likes and dislikes.

Brainstorm and write down as many questions as you can. Don't just develop questions for each topic once: Do each topic over and over again, just like baseball players practice hitting the ball over and over again.

You can do the same thing if you and all of your peers work from home. You would need to use video conferencing or simple conference calls. This is possible, but you will need to get everybody to commit to focus and not do email and other things during the practice, or it will be as boring as your boss's staff meeting.

> Practice every skill: the ones you have and the ones you still need.

Make adjustments in the structure all the time; try to make it fun, but effective. This is a money party where everybody must understand it is their job to make it a time-worthy experience.

Be creative. Using the lessons of the previous chapters of this book, but also the knowledge of who you are, develop practice plans to scrimmage likeability, trust, and influence. You should have a practice plan for every conceivable skill you use in professional sales.

## PRACTICE: 25% - PRIORITIZING PRACTICE

We all believe that if you really want to improve at *playing* golf, you have to *regularly practice*. Some people will even tell you that you will need a professional trainer or coach in order to become better.

WE PRIORITIZE PRACTICE ELSEWHERE, SO...

For those of us who are parents, we encourage our children to practice. We may even demand it. I know I instruct my kids to practice at the sports that they play regularly. I'm even willing to put in the extra gas mileage and spend part of my busy day to get my kids to and from practice. Our commitment to the sport involves the same commitment to the practices as to the games.

When we are sitting in our comfortable chairs watching a sporting event on TV, we sometimes comment on how a professional athlete is not playing up to his or her normal standard (and does not deserve the money he or she is making) because he or she did not practice during training camp.

All of this is to say that we all really recognize the importance of practice, even if we don't think its importance applies to us. What we need to realize is that the need to practice does apply to us in our business. We sales professionals must master some of the most difficult skills in any industry, and yet we typically practice the least of any skills-based business professionals.

### GIVING YOUR BEST IS NEVER REGRETTABLE

Some people are shocked when I remark that salesmanship is one of the hardest skills in any profession. The fact is that salesmanship is an art form comprised of intangibles like attitudes, egos, emotions, and energy. Great salesmanship requires discernment and the ability to adapt to situations beyond the control of the sales professional.

What would happen to a sports team that practiced as often as sales teams do? What will happen to a sales team the practices like a winning sports team?

It is not by coincidence that the sales departments of most companies have the highest compensated employees. While the steps required to sell are relatively simple, selling itself is not. Yet, most sales teams are not given the opportunity to practice once a month, if even once a year.

Imagine if a professional sports team, like the Dallas Cowboys, used the corporate sales "practicing strategy." Players would practice the first week of their first year and never practice again. The coach would say, "Troy Aikman does not need to practice. He has been throwing the football since he was a kid; he has been playing football for the Cowboys for eight years now. I just leave him alone and let him do his job on game day." Wouldn't we think the head coach had lost his mind? And after having a season of losing every game, he most assuredly would get fired.

Does this example sound unrealistic? It shouldn't. Many corporate sales leaders have said to me, when I've asked about training their sales people, "Oh, Nathan, most of my sales people have been here over 10 years and have been selling for more years than that. They don't need the practice you're suggesting." Yeah, they do. Not because they're necessarily poor sellers, but because of the simple truth that everyone from the golfer to the writer to the musician to the sales professional must continue to *practice* to *improve* and to *win*.

> Unpracticed skills vanish like a lost sale.

The fundamental reason why all of these professionals need to practice is that these jobs make use of skills, and skills are things that we're either getting better at or getting worse at. No skill remains static.

A trumpet player who forsakes the instrument for years cannot just pick it up later and play with the same skill. A writer who spends months away from the keyboard will find the right words more elusive. The student of a foreign language who avoids study over the summer will return to school with a smaller vocabulary and less competence with the grammar.

Skills necessitate practice. That's their nature. Use them or lose them. As sales is a skills-heavy profession, the sales professional must practice to develop—and maintain—those skills. I'm not just making a neat-sounding analogy between sales professionals and athletes. There is a real similarity between the two professions: both use skills and so both must practice to be successful. And if done well, both professions can lead to oodles of money.

Remember that there's a key difference between practicing and playing the game. While you use skills and will to an extent develop them while playing the game, the intent of the game is not to build skills. You're not focusing on getting better at skill A or skill B while concentrating on the game, so your development of the skills will be more incidental. In practice, however, your intent and attention are aimed at skill development, so your improvement of them will accelerate at full throttle.

## PRACTICE: 50% - COMMITMENT TO GETTING BETTER

When I was a young boy and the prospect of selling to prospective customers was still beyond the horizon, I was developing some of the very skills I would later use in my sales profession. I played sports.

> Scrimmaging is role-playing with the right intent. It is therefore enjoyable!

My favorite part of playing sports was playing the game, of course, but the only time I enjoyed practice was when we scrimmaged. To me, it was like playing the game without consequences. The same could be said in sales; we love the sales call but hate the role-playing. We discussed this heavily in another chapter, but it is important enough to discuss again. Role-playing is sometimes used to test knowledge, to show off, or, regrettably, to see someone fail. The wrong intent is used. As a sales professional you need to take it upon yourself to *scrimmage*—to role play with the right intent.

### IT'S TIME TO SCRIMMAGE

Scrimmage every week or even every day if you can. *Scrimmaging should be fun*. The intent of the scrimmage is not to prove what you know; rather, it is to try new things or really look at how you can improve on a skill or a part of the sales call.

The next time you have an appointment, do a scrimmage with a peer that you respect and ask him or her to be honest with you and give you constructive feedback. Scrimmage a second time if you need to. Try this just once and see if it makes a difference. I guarantee, if done with the right intent, it will.

Just the other day my brother was going for a job interview and, because he was a great fit for it, he really wanted the job. So for several weeks before the interview we conducted several scrimmages together, and with each scrimmage he got better. He went on to four interviews with this company and he *got* the job. He had practiced for the game, and because he had practiced, he played much better than he would have otherwise.

If I told you that scrimmaging prospecting calls, asking for referrals, and asking understanding questions would increase your sales 50% over the next 12 months, would you do it? I hope so.

### BE COACHABLE

> The superstar athletes have no qualms about being coached. Why should you?

So many times, we as sales professional love to say we want to learn or be coached, but deep down inside we feel that because we have been selling so long and have been to hundreds of selling skills trainings, we've got it all and really don't need any more coaching. Feeling this way is the biggest disservice you could do to yourself.

Remember the acts of coaching and practicing are not the same as training or learning a new *trick*: they involve getting better at the things you already know and possibly gaining new *skills*.

If you still feel that you don't need any additional learning, why buy or read any books on sales including this one? You should call the local funeral home and order your casket ahead of time because you, I regret to say, are dying in your field.

Several years back I had a sales rep who was a good producer—not great, but good. He was a know-it-all and bragged to everybody about all that he knew. He was not confident—he was arrogant. After several months we had had several meetings on his unwillingness to be coached, as I really wanted to see him lose the attitude and gain an even higher position of success.

At any rate, I eventually sat down with him and told him that although his results were good, I found his inability to learn and his lack of desire to be coached a reason to find opportunity elsewhere. Sadly enough I think he was found to be selling discounted pictures to some of my office mates a few years later.

He was good, as I said, but because he refused to practice, he didn't stay good. His performance got worse with time. We see this in sports all the time: a super star with a bad attitude or who is un-coachable is traded to a different team each year. Soon enough no one wants him.

Sell your ego and be coachable; you will be amazed of how much better even the best sales professional can become.

## HIT THE GROUND RUNNING

A sales practice program is not difficult to create. However, it will take great discipline and coaching to make it a long-term and effective program. Being a sales leader is not about title; it is about behavior. This focus on behavior is sometimes lost in sales because of the culture prevalent in many sales organizations, and also because of us, the sales professionals.

You cannot get beyond peak without practice. Without practice, hitting peak means going down.

Some top sales producers are more likely prima donnas than sales leaders. They feel they don't need to practice; the sales leaders don't scrimmage with them because they feel that they know what they are doing. This is truly sad because a sales professional eventually hits a peak and all they have left to do is go down. Rookies dedicated to regular practice rise to their places. Even worse, some of these former top performers leave the company instead of starting to practice. Everyone loses.

I see it all the time: you have a sales professional who was number one for several years, but because he or she had been able to live on referrals and not had to practice or be challenged, the numbers slowly declined each year. The sales professional in this situation has to make a decision: lose the ego and start to practice, learn and focus, or leave the company and start over. Most often such professionals don't lose their ego. The company loses, and so does the sales professional, but where the company's loss is short term, the individual's loss is long term.

## WHEN IN DOUBT, PUNT

In business today, we cannot control the economy, competitive pressures, and whatever bad news the media is talking about. However, we can control our selling skills and how good we are as sales professionals.

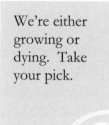

We're either growing or dying. Take your pick.

Remember, as with everything else on this planet, you are either growing or you are dying. Don't be the one to call the funeral home and don't give others a reason to call for you. Just because you have been doing a job for a long time does not mean you cannot improve.

Despite the sport and business commonalities, as sales professionals, we do not get paid to *play* a game, we get paid to *work*. You owe it to yourself, your family, and your team to practice and achieve the financial and personal success you deserve.

## Chapter Eight Highlights

- Sports teams spend 90% of the time practicing and 10% of the time playing the game. In business, we spend less than 1% of the time practicing and 99% of the time playing the game.

- Selling is simple, but not easy.

- Skills demand more than playing the game. They demand practice. Otherwise, they disappear.

- Develop a practice plan that builds your skills—both short-term and long-term.

- Stay committed to getting better.

# 9

# BUILDING YOUR
# PROSPECT PIPELINE

pros·pect  (ˈprä-spekt) n. 1. *A potential customer or client*

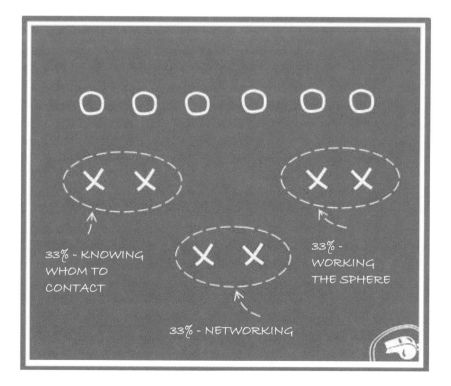

Think back to your high school and college days. Did you ever know the type of person who waited around for friendships to form or romantic engagements to fall from the sky? Instead of getting out of the house or dorm room to meet people, these shy folks hung out alone, waiting quietly in their rooms with sporadic glances at their silent phones.

If they ventured into public, they sat by themselves in the cafeteria or the student lounge, waiting to be noticed. They weren't in short supply of desire for companionship, but they went about trying to build relationships in all the wrong ways. In most cases, they simply lacked the courage to say "Hi" to new people or sit at an occupied table in the café. A little dose of extrovert juice would have transformed their entire social life. They didn't need a magic potion; they just needed to speak.

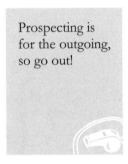

Prospecting is for the outgoing, so go out!

Why do I mention these shy, longing types? So I can tell you not to be like them when looking for business. You can't have a seat at your desk with Outlook open and the phone by your side and expect calls and emails to hit you like a hail storm. Not unless you've first gotten out there and established relationships with new prospects.

Establishing relationships with prospects does take energy and time. You have to talk to strangers, ask questions, answer their questions, and tell them about yourself, what you do, and what you can offer them. And you have to do this without waiting for solicitations. You cannot wait for the introductions; you must make the introductions.

In this chapter, we'll cover the principles and strategies for building an effective prospect pipeline or prospect sphere. We'll first look at who you should be contacting and how you can build a promising prospect sphere. Second, we'll examine a variety of networking tools and how you can make the most of them. Third, we'll explore how to most effectively work your prospect sphere.

# PROSPECTING: 33% - KNOWING WHOM TO CONTACT

You probably don't need me to tell you that the old school technique of "dialing for dollars" is not the best way to prospect. Calling each entry in the phonebook and asking for the person who handles the products and services you sell won't yield you nearly as many hits as other prospecting methods.

Nevertheless, I will say that if you don't have a qualified list or some warm prospects yet, then get to dialing. It's better than nothing, and if you just sit and wait for the phone to ring, you will undoubtedly end up with some serious chair sores and zero prospects to show for the aches and pains.

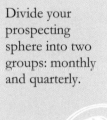

Divide your prospecting sphere into two groups: monthly and quarterly.

Let's not settle for mediocrity, though. The true sales professional has an effective plan for identifying prospects to call and developing a solid prospect sphere.

## GET PERMISSION TO MAKE THE CALL

Building a sphere is a key practice in any sales organization, no matter the industry, and whether the selling involves business-to-business or business-to-consumer. Your prospect sphere is comprised of a group of prospects you communicate with on a regular basis. They have potential to buy things from you or refer business to you, and they have given you permission to call them on a regular basis. Yes, I said *their permission.*

Getting the prospect's permission to call is the key aspect of building a great prospect pipeline. Many times sales people will have their pipeline full of potential sales or suspects. I use the word "suspects" because in many cases the sales person has never spoken to the suspect. Maybe the sales professional has left numerous messages or thinks seeing the company name on a sign somewhere is sufficient.

If you are leaving messages for suspects and prospects, and they never call you back, they are probably not viable. (We will discuss how to get people to call you back in the next chapter tele-prospecting).

The goal of all prospecting—whether you use a target list, lead company, referrals, networking, or plain cold calling—is to get the prospects' permission to call them on a regular basis. By regular I mean monthly or maybe quarterly if they are a smaller opportunity.

The pipeline becomes the source for your new clients, so treat it as such. This idea is not new, and it is not complicated, but too often we start skipping it or simply go through the motions when we prospect.

My sphere is divided into two groups: monthly and quarterly. One list I contact on a monthly basis, and the other I call on a quarterly basis. I make this division based on the number of prospects I have in my pipeline, so I can prioritize my calls as the pipeline grows.

If prospects insist I not call them monthly, I then ask if they'd agree to a quarterly call. My personal goal is to have one hundred people in my monthly sphere and fifty people in my quarterly sphere, but you should determine the goal that works best for you. We discuss the details of how to work the sphere later in the chapter.

### WHO'S ON FIRST?

To begin your sphere, find the best calls, your most promising prospects, and start with these. Who is likely to give you new business? What about repeat business? Who is likely to refer people to you? Jot down these names and numbers. Now.

Note: these prospects are *not* your friends and family. Often times when a sales professional starts a new job or starts a new business, he or she looks to friends and family to be the first customers. BAD IDEA.

Trust me when I tell you more often than not, your friends and family will be the last ones that will buy from you. In the long run, this is a good thing. Don't rely on friends and family to be your first customers, and then you will be forced to start looking for a strategic and sustainable prospect list.

> You can't rely on friends and family to build a successful prospect sphere.

Salespeople who depend on friends and family for business don't stay in sales.

So, after you've begun the sphere, how do you build a strategic and sustainable sphere? First, identify who your target market is. Second, identify the companies and contact people in those target markets. Third, start to find ways to get in contact with them.

Note these means of communication in your sphere. They may include networking, phone calls, visiting offices, attending trade shows, following your dollar, and others.

There many ways you can take these steps, but I will share with you a couple ways that have worked well for my teams. If you think of other ways, try them!

## PROSPECTING: 33% - NETWORKING

If you are in B-to-B sales, I suggest building your own networking group. You can do this by finding four or five other business-to-business sales professionals that sell to your same target market. For example, if I sold Telecom, then I would find top sales professionals in office supplies sales, a marketing company or advertising company, wireless sales, business machines, and office rental.

There are tons of business-to-business sales professionals, and every one of them has the same goal: find a way to gain more prospects.

Networking in unison nets you more prospects than you would catch on your own.

Make this an elite group; do not just take anybody who wants to join. I think of a networking group as a money party; I am not looking for a social group or more non-revenue generating friends.

I am looking for like-minded sales professionals to build a group that will help all of us grow our businesses. I want committed professionals who bring something new and advantageous to the group.

One of the best programs I have seen for networking groups is BNI (Business Networking International). While I have found most BNI groups tend to focus on business-to-consumer, you can find those that focus on business-to-business.

Accept only the best in your networking group.

In 2006 I was looking to join a BNI group to help me grow the mortgage business we owned at the time. I looked around but was less than impressed with the groups I visited. It was not that I thought I was better; I was just looking for a group with a little more to offer. After a few months of searching, my wife suggested we start our own group. As it was my wife making the suggestion, I wisely agreed, as I always do.

When we started this group, we did not want just anybody; we wanted impressive sales professionals. We sought the best of the best. Today we are no longer in this group, but my former mortgage partner still is, and to this day it is one of the strongest groups in the city helping each sales professional in the group gain market share and grow revenue.

Network marketing is about helping other people, and if everyone helps each other, than you can have x amount of people being PR agents on your behalf (the x depends on the number of members).

It's a potluck party of prospects, and everyone needs to bring a unique and complementary dish.

TRADE SHOWS AND TRADESHOW BOOKS

I once worked with a client in the trade show business, and we would encourage the sales professionals to use the tradeshow books as a calling database. These books list qualified buyers who were participants of several tradeshows throughout the year.

If you attend tradeshows in any industry, use these books to build your prospect sphere. Your competitors will be using them as well, so it may be difficult to reach the people listed, but fewer sales professionals use these than you might think, and I know from experience that sales professionals who take advantage of the tradeshow lists have the strongest closes.

The ones who don't use them may be successful in their own right, but they'd be even more successful if they use the tools right underneath their noses. Too often we have "the list" and the tools in front of us, but we don't use them to the fullest (if at all).

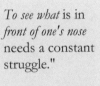

*To see what* is in *front of one's nose* needs a constant struggle."

- George Orwell.

Of course, trade shows avail you with more than just books. There are steps you can take to make the most of them. Keep in mind these steps are applicable whether you sell widgets, chopping knives, or nuclear atom constructors.

**Step 1:** Call all clients your company may have at an upcoming tradeshow and see if they need anything, and let them know you will be at the show if they do need something later.

**Step 2:** Ask them if they know of anyone else going to the show that they feel could use your help.

**Step 3:** Call forty vendors a day to see if they need anything for the show, and if not, ask if you could stop by and introduce yourself at the show. The goal of this would be to set up ten to twelve introductions for you to do at the upcoming trade show.

**Step 4:** Go to the show and visit your current customers and your ten to twelve new introductions.

**Step 5:** Call each contact you made (current and new) after the show to touch base and see how the show went.

**Step 6:** If any qualify as a good prospective customer, ask if you can call them to stay in touch. This builds your sphere.

This is not just calling a list: it is a whole program to build your sales funnel. Using this simple process, find events that your target market participates in and develop a plan to interact and start building relationships. The ultimate goal is to either make a sale or add a qualified prospect to my "Permission Sphere."

## CHAMBER OF COMMERCE

I love the Chamber of Commerce, and I think they do a lot of good things for the business community. However, I have found that the chamber is not a very effective networking tool. The reason I say this is if you have ever been to a mixer or meeting, it is mostly a lot of sales people trying to sell each other, or worse, new business owners trying to figure life out (which is OK, just not a revenue generator).

> "To succeed in sales, simply talk to lots of people each day. And here's what's exciting – there are lots of people!"
>
> - Jim Rohn

Please don't misunderstand: business *can* happen at the chamber. But almost anyone can be a member, and you don't want just anyone in your network. I think the Chamber can provide knowledge and comradeship, as well as help build relationships, but ultimately is a very weak lead generator. I am sure there are people who believe that the Chamber is the place to go for business, and more power to them, but if you work for me, I will tell you that you will not hit quota using the Chamber.

## BUSINESS CONTACTS AND NETWORKING WITH FRIENDS

This is a no brainer: anytime you know someone who can introduce you to a person who can benefit from your product or service, then do it—talk to him or her. Remember to take care of your friends who introduced you, and they may just do it again.

I am not telling you to sell to your friends and family; I am saying ask your friends for their help in pointing you in the direction of someone who may need your services or products, and do your best to return the favor when you can. I have called on my friends many times in my career and still do. A phone of one of my friends is probably ringing right now.

Of course, while this avenue is a no brainer, it shouldn't be your only means of networking. Use it, but don't rely on it. Remember: you cannot depend on friends and family to stay in business.

## FOLLOW YOUR DOLLAR

"Following your dollar" is another great way to help grow your contacts. Following your dollar is very simple: it means wherever you spend money, tell people what you do for a living. The theory is if you spend money somewhere, someday these places may spend money with you.

> How many ways can you tell people what you do for a living?

You can see signs of "following your dollar" at local car washes, lube centers and other businesses where they have a corkboard with people's cards tacked to it. I applaud their efforts, but I don't know anyone making a living by putting cards up in the local carwash; however, it's not hard and it doesn't take much time, so feel free to do it.

There are better methods of following your dollar, however. A lady had her children enrolled in my wife's art studio, and a few months later my wife hosted an event for her company to help sell her product. The joint venture helped both businesses and introduced new prospects to each of them.

Where do you spend money? Could they benefit from what you sell? Could their other customers (in a way that doesn't compete)? If so, tell them what you do for a living.

Wherever you go, be proud of what you do and let people know about it. If you suddenly think of ways your business and the business of another could benefit one another, bring it up.

## PROSPECTING: 33% - WORKING THE SPHERE

Sales is said to be a relationship business, and yet many sales professionals are not willing to invest in a relationship until the client invests in them. The reverse should be the case; sales professionals need to invest in a relationship before a client will invest in them. This does not mean we have to buy them lunch once a month or spend a ton of time or money on them; investing here just takes a phone conversation and some nuggets of valuable information.

Relationships in sales tend to get rocky. It's sad, but true. Sometime within a six month period, your competition will do something wrong, and that will be the day you happen to call that prospect. The prospect will share how he or she is upset with the current supplier and will ask if you can visit to discuss *your* product or service.

Several years ago, when I was a sales professional, I was making a sphere call to someone that I had been calling every month for a period of six months. In fact, the first time I called her, she said that it was not necessary to call every month (it might not have been that nice), but I promised her that I would keep it short and that I would not hound her about gaining her business. I just wanted to check in each month to see how she was doing. She eventually agreed.

Keep in regular contact with your prospects. Touch base and say "Hi."

So I called Debra on this particular Thursday, expecting to have our similar conversation about her upcoming weekend plans and just overall touching base. Instead she tells me that she just hung up with her current provider, and that they had just really made her exasperated and mad.

She said to me, "Today is your lucky day, Nathan. Can you come out tomorrow and show me what you have to offer and what you can do to make me happy?" Of course, busy as I was, I told her that I was booked, but that I would move some things around and could be there by 3:00 pm the following day. Two weeks later I had a new customer.

I always kept my calls very personable and not very "salesy." I didn't call from an angle of pushing a sale or future business. I just touched base with my potential prospects, and that proved enough to keep me in their minds when they suddenly needed my services.

## COMING UP WITH THE PLAYS

When you meet a qualified prospect who has not purchased from you, ask if you can stay in contact—on a monthly basis if the prospect is a candidate for your product or service. If the prospect tells you that it is not necessary, say something like, "I find that sales is a relationship business, and much of my success has been based on me investing in the relationship before I ask a client to invest in me. I promise I will keep it short and I won't hound you to buy my product. I just want to say hello and touch base. Would that be ok with you?"

I like to use some humor, but I recommend you use your own personality. By the way, leaving a voice mail does not count; you can't build a relationship by leaving messages. Leave the relationships with machines to the science fiction movies.

*Helpful hint:* If you need a reason to call, send the prospect a little nugget in an email and so that when you call, you can double check if they received your email. There are many things you can do to create a reason to call, and all are fine as long as they are honest and help you make the call.

## THE STANDINGS IN THE GAME

The numbers are not magic, but they help you gauge what you need to do to reach your goal. If I wanted ten sales a month and I found that 10% of the people I called would eventually lead to a close, then I knew I had to call at least one hundred people. Easy math. I have never seen a sales professional with a 100-person sphere miss quota.

> I have never seen a sales professional with a 100-person sphere miss quota.

The percentages may vary depending on your industry or business, but the principles are the same.

The more prospects you can put into your pipeline, the more likely you will be to make and exceed quota. Just as your grandma had her magic recipe for those delicious cookies, you need to know the recipe to obtain your sales goals.

The magic question: How many prospects does a sales professional need in the pipeline? The answer will vary by company or industry. In my organization, I liked to see my sales people with three times their monthly goal (prospects) in their current pipeline.

To give a quick break down of numbers from pipeline to sales, you can look at this formula: If my goal is $100,000 in monthly sales revenue, and my average sale was $10,000, then I need on average ten sales each month to reach my goal.

In most cases in sales, the revenue per sale can vary drastically, but in most cases an experienced sales professional who knows the industry can come up with a pretty accurate average.

Formula:

- 10 sales (average sale of $10,000 for a total of $100,000)
- 30 working prospects in the pipeline (based on 1/3 of my monthly goal)
- 100 total prospects in the funnel (based on a minimum of three times my monthly need)
- 20 appointments (based on a close ratio of 50%)
- 150 prospects per week (based on 1 out of 30 calls setting an appointment)

It is not important that your formula is the same as the example I gave you, but what is important is that you have a formula that will work for you. Building a formula is about understanding what needs to be done to ensure success, so be conservative in your conversion ratios. Better to have more sales than not enough sales!

### THE BENEFIT

Prospect strategies are like strands on a web: the more you have, the sturdier the web, and if one strategy is low, the others keep the web in place. In other words, there are many avenues to build your prospect funnel.

I've discussed starting elite networking groups, utilizing tradeshows, using the Chamber of Commerce, helping friends, and "following the dollar," but there are many others, and you may come up with your own.

Some strategies will work well for you, and some may not. This is dependant not only on your industry, your market, your demographic, but also on *you*. Like everything we talk about in sales, nothing happens over night, so you have to stay committed to it before you will find that the prospects start committing to you.

Your prospect pipeline isn't there as a record of your calls, but as a plan to work continuously. To make your prospect pipeline work for you, you need to be committed to it—committed to keeping in touch with your prospects. Over time they may cease to be prospects and become your customers and clients, but only if you stay organized, focused, and committed.

## CHAPTER NINE HIGHLIGHTS

- A sphere is a group of prospects you communicate with on a regular basis that have potential to buy from you or refer business to you.

- Do not sell to your friends and family.

- You will not build your business through the Chamber.

- Follow your dollar.

- Prospect strategies are like strands on a web: the more you have, the sturdier the web, and if one strategy is low, the others keep the web in place.

# 10

# TELE-PROSPECTING

pros·pect·ing ('prä-spek-tiŋ) n. 1. *Pursuing prospects*

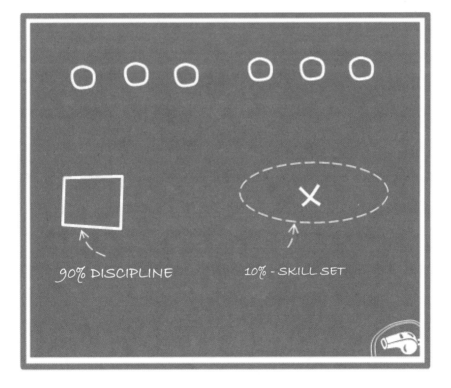

Regardless of where your prospects come from—vertical markets, industry contacts, referrals, Google search engines, trade magazines, etc.—you still have to *make the calls*.

Like all prospecting, tele-prospecting stinks like an infant's diaper. It is the worst part of any sales job. It's tedious and its rewards are not immediately apparent. It doesn't provide instant gratification and usually delivers frustration after frustration, gift-wrapped in yesterday's diapers. A small percentage of calls yield results. And yet those results matter and make the tediousness worth it.

> "[Perseverance] overcomes almost anything, even nature."
>
> - John D. Rockefeller

You'll never get any results without picking up the phone and making the calls. The more you can do it, the more successful you will be. In fact, *sales professionals that prospect religiously will typically be the highest paid* sales professionals in the organization.

When potential sales professionals that tell me that they love to prospect, I tell them that they are either crazy or lying to me. I know there are people out there that don't mind it, but to say you love it is, well, kind of creepy. I don't mind changing diapers, but you'd rightly wonder about me if I said I loved it.

Prospecting is to sales professionals what spring training camp is to football players, or the bar exam is to lawyers, or what residency is to doctors. It makes playing the game possible. Face it: you can't dance the tango without a partner, deliver a baby without a mother, prosecute without an accused, or tackle without a player holding the football. You can't sell without prospects.

The more focused you are and the more effort you put into these requirements, the more successful you will be. So embrace it because prospecting is 90% discipline and 10% skill set, but *100% necessary*.

# PROSPECTING: 90% - DISCIPLINE

Tele-prospecting is dead. I read that in a restroom somewhere. I also see advertisements all the time for ways to get new prospects without having to tele-market or make cold calls. It seems like everybody and their smart phone has a new and improved system that will make customers flock to your doors and buy your product or service. Sign me up for all of them with a money back guarantee. The only thing I will get is my money back.

I don't believe there is a surefire way to get an appointment without making a call. Whether you use social media, networking, referrals or lead generation tools, you need to make a phone call eventually to prospect effectively. Yes, technology is advancing faster than ever, but a text message or an IM is no substitute for a phone call where prospecting is concerned.

> "Discipline is the bridge between goals and accomplishment."
>
> - Jim Rohn

Many small businesses fail because owners and operators fail to prospect. Perhaps they naively believe that because they're experts and know their industry, customers will find them. Perhaps they don't know how to prospect or, worse, don't care to learn. Whatever the case, without prospecting, they are no prospects. Without prospects there are no customers, and without customers, there's no business.

## THE GOOD AND THE BAD OF TELE-PROSPECTING

I prefer doing phone call prospecting to doing in-person prospecting, although that's just me, and I can and do both. Like anything, though, it has its upsides and downsides.

The chief benefit of tele-prospecting is time. I can make an average of twenty calls in an hour. It could take all day and a full tank of gas to make 20 in-person cold calls. Don't get me wrong: I have seen many sales professionals, including professionals on my team, do great by doing in-person cold calling.

Another benefit: tele-prospecting doesn't hurt as much if you are rejected—you don't feel like you've intruded by walking into someone's business. Plus it's easier to hang up and make the next call than it is to knock on the next door after the receptionist kicks you out while pointing to the "No Soliciting" sign on the door. Calling someone is more personal than sending the person an email or letter, but it's still distant enough that rejection doesn't hit as hard.

> Everything has its upside and downside.

Of course, tele-prospecting has is downside. Did I mention it stinks? It is easy to be rejected. Reaching the prospect often means contending with the prospect's human or digital gate keeper. It is very easy to get distracted and not make the calls.

As we do with anything that has pros and cons (and what doesn't?), we sales professionals must allow the positives to motivate us and create disciplines and programs to eliminate or minimize the negatives. Let's look at some of these disciplines.

## MAKE THE TIME

There is a simple rule of getting things done and that is to do what you like the least *first*. Following that logic, I make all of my prospecting calls first thing in the morning. If I try and do them after lunch or at the end of the day, I'm tempted to give a million and one reasons why I am not able to make the calls until the next day.

Excuses to avoid calling come easy. They can range from customer service issues and running out of time to the electricity going out and lightening striking your spouse's poodle. Whatever the excuse and however seemingly legitimate, the bottom line is you didn't make the calls to prospect for business.

Making the time means scheduling it. For example, put down in your schedule that every Monday through Thursday you are going to make a minimum of forty prospecting calls from 8:00 am to 10:00 am. If you end up having some long conversations, then great, keep the momentum up and keep going! If you leave forty voicemails and you are done by 9:00 am, *then call more people*. The sales process is not complicated: to get sales you must have appointments and to get appointments you must obtain qualified prospects. So call them!

## Make the Time, Rainmakers!

All sales departments have rainmakers. Rainmakers are individuals that bring in large amounts of revenue. A note for you successful rainmakers out there: don't stop making rain so you can bucket it, make more rain and hire people to bucket it. You will surely have your dry spells, maybe even times when rookies outperform you. If you don't make the time to prospect, you will stop making rain. Stop making rain, and you'll find yourself faced with two options: 1) lose your badge of honor by starting over or 2) keep your pride by starting over elsewhere, in another organization. Everyone loses in either case, so don't stop prospecting when the rain is falling.

> Don't stop prospecting just because you've reached a peak.

## Schedule Prospecting as You Would an Appointment

The key to making the time is to treat prospecting not as something to fit in your schedule if you can just find a space, but rather as you would a customer appointment or a meeting with your boss. You would not cancel tomorrow's appointment with a prospective customer so that you can respond to email or handle customer issues, so why do it to your prospecting "appointment"?

Now let's address the little voice in your head that's asking, "What if I have a customer that can only meet between the hours of 8:00 am to 10:00 am?" If this is really the case (and I mean *really* the case), here is what I would do: I'd tell the customer I have an appointment at that time, *because I do*, and I would attempt to meet after 10:00 am. If that were truly not an option, I would let the customer know that I will work on moving some things around and will contact them back shortly. Before I actually book the appointment, I would move the prospecting time directly after the appointment I am scheduling. I would reschedule the prospecting time just as I would any other important appointment.

You have to schedule prospecting even if your calendar is full of appointments. Would you not schedule an important appointment because you've got a full plate? Of course not. You'd make the time. So make the time for prospecting.

If you make the time and don't make excuses, you will find your disciplines will become second nature and your sales *will* increase.

CONSISTENT PROSPECTING CREATES CONSISTENT SALES

"Sales have peaks and valleys." Ever hear this? See it written at some seminar? This is a true statement, but peaks and valleys are self-inflicted. Think about it. I would bet depending on your sales cycle, that your peaks and valleys follow a similar trend.

Prospecting season lasts year round.

Here is what happens: we spend a month prospecting heavily and going on new appointments. We spend the next month going on follow up appointments, preparing proposals and closing deals in which we did not have time to prospect for further appointments. The following month we are delivering products or implementing our services, and again we had no time to prospect. So at last the following month our pipeline is empty, and we spend the month prospecting with nothing in the pipeline and therefore little to no sales. And then the cycle starts over again.

The way to solve this is to be like a farmer and plant seeds every season—only for sales professionals *every day is a new season*. The peaks and valleys become only peaks if we keep our 8:00 am to 10:00 am prospecting time.

A lot of sales reps tell me this talk of scheduled prospecting sounds great, but in the real world it is just not possible. But I *am* talking real world. That is the world I know, the world in which I have been a successful sales professional. I know it's possible because I've done it. I have no capacity for the impossible; I'm not Superman, no matter what my children say.

Moreover, this prospecting schedule is a must to keep growing business. Let me say it another way: if I told you I would double your income from last year and all you had to do was call prospects every day from 8:00 am to 10:00 am, would you do it? But here is the caveat: if you miss one day of your two hour prospecting schedule, I cancel the deal. What are the chances you would not make those calls? Slim to none unless you didn't want to double your income, right? And if that is the case, you don't need to read this book or any other, because you fall into the "I don't need to learn or grow" category of salespeople.

> An effective prospecting schedule IS POSSIBLE!

## PROSPECTING: 10% - SKILL SET

Here's an all too common scenario: Fred, a seasoned sales rep, gets to the office first thing in the morning, sips his flavor-of-the-day coffee, flirts with Wilma by the copy machine, trying to impress her with something new to talk about, and then, when it's time to start calling prospects, sits at his desk, makes a call, and leaves the same old voicemail for a prospective client he always leaves.

Fred varies his coffee, his topics of conversation with colleagues, and the witty lines he delivers to impress Wilma; but when calling prospects, he never varies the message and rarely varies his tone or inflection.

Even worse, after leaving the message, he schedules the follow-up call for the following month. He wouldn't dare follow-up a call to Wilma a month after leaving a message, but this practice seems perfectly suitable to him when trying to reach prospects.

Would you follow-up with your boss a month after a conversation? Of course not. So why do so with a prospect?

This practice keeps him active, but doesn't yield him results. His prospects receive hundreds of calls each month, and so none of them remember Fred's message when he calls back the next month. Fred calls so infrequently that his prospects can easily ignore him and just hope he goes away.

Ignoring Fred works well for his prospects. While most people hate getting rejected, they hate rejecting others even more. Everyone knows someone who wants to break up with his or her significant other, but doesn't want to do the rejecting, so instead tries to make the other so mad that the other does the breaking up.

Prospects don't like rejecting sales people any more than people like rejecting potential boyfriends or girlfriends. A prospect would rather ignore the salesperson than reject him. Fred helps his prospects do just that.

### THE 3X48 PROGRAM

Here's where tele-prospecting, or what I like to call the 3x48 program, comes in. The 3x48 program will not only put an end to the scenario above, but it will move the process along and allow a sales professional to move the prospect up to being a possible client or out of the call rotation altogether. Here is how it works:

The sales professional makes three calls, each one 48 hours apart. For example: The first call on Monday, the second on Wednesday and the third on Friday. Each call has a different goal, and each is a step to get the prospect to return the call.

**Call Number One:**

The goal of the first call is to introduce yourself to the prospective client and ask him or her to call you back. Here's an example:

"Hello, my name is Fred Smith and I'm with Ziggurat Sales Development. The reason for my call is to introduce myself to you and to offer you a free business analysis of your 2011 sales plans. We have helped many clients increase their profits in difficult and changing markets. I would greatly appreciate it if you would call me back at this number... Thanks and have a wonderful day."

**Call Number Two:**

The goal of the second call is to let the prospect know you are following up to the call you left a couple days ago.

"Hello Mr. Prospect my name is Fred Smith with Ziggurat Sales Development. I left you a message a couple days ago and wanted to follow up with you regarding your free business analysis. Again my phone number is... Thanks again and I look forward to hearing from you soon."

**Call Number Three:**

The goal of the third call is to let the prospect know you are not trying to pester him, and give him permission to reject you (this call is key).

> Give the prospect permission to reject you. This makes the prospect more comfortable.

"Hello Mr. Prospect, this is Fred Smith with Ziggurat Sales Development. I know I left you a couple messages this week and don't mean to be overbearing, but I want to make sure I do a good job following up and let you know that I would love the opportunity to visit for a few minutes. I was hoping you would do me a favor and let me know if either (A) you would like to talk to me but you have just been too busy, or (B) you don't feel it would be a good time for us to meet and would prefer that I don't call again. I know your time is valuable and I would appreciate your direction as to how to proceed next. Thanks again and have a wonderful day."

This three-call method is successful because:

- The calls are close enough to each other that the prospect remembers you (after the third call, they definitely know who you are).

- The prospect starts to think that if he or she doesn't call you back you may never stop calling.

- You gave the prospect permission to reject you, so he or she feels more comfortable calling you back.

- You are assertive but not aggressive. Your calls are consistent and direct, but not generic or too "salesy."

## ANALYZING THE PROBLEM

If you are not getting the number of appointments you need, simply making more calls may not be the answer. You need to understand where you are losing traction.

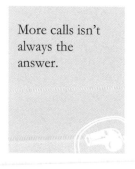

More calls isn't always the answer.

If a person were trying to improve their golf swing, a golf coach isn't going to tell him or her to just keep swinging the club. No, you must stop to see where the problems are in the swing and then work them out one at a time.

If you are making 60 calls a day, leaving 50 voicemails and no one is calling you back, then look at who you are calling or what your message sounds like. Are you following up frequently? Are you encouraging your prospects to ignore you?

## SCRIMMAGE THOSE SKILLS

Here is an opportunity to go to your sales leader and get him or her to help you. Scrimmage prospecting calls with your leader, or at least with fellow sales professionals, and get the outside perspectives on where you can improve.

Calling prospects is a skill. It takes practice to master. Start by implementing the three-step calling method, the 3x48 program I outlined above. Don't just put it into practice; practice it in your scrimmages. You don't get the opportunity to revise your voicemails, and even if you did, you don't have the time. Get to the point where leaving effective voicemails becomes second nature. But be sure to keep prospecting in your practice regiment even after you've got the skill down.

## Chapter Ten Highlights

- You are going to have to make calls no matter where your business comes from.

- Tele-prospecting is 90% discipline, 10% skill, but 100% necessary.

- Do first what you like least.

- Treat prospecting as you treat prospective customer appointments.

- Implement and practice the 3x48 program.

# 11

# THE GOLDEN T

gold·en ('gōl-dən) adj. 1. *Having a promising feature; seemingly assured of success*

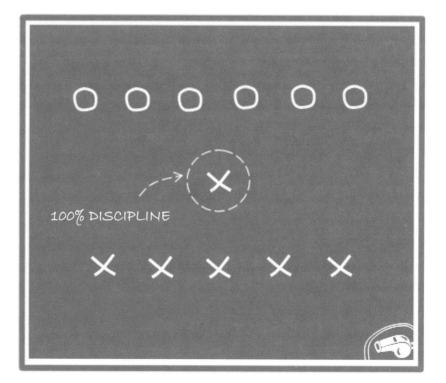

You have the chance to turn every one of your appointments into *three* new opportunities.

One of the biggest mistakes sales professionals make is going to their appointments and then leaving to go back to the office or just go on to their next appointment.

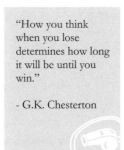

"How you think when you lose determines how long it will be until you win."

- G.K. Chesterton

While I am not a fan of driving around town walking up and down floors of an office building to make cold calls, I do know that many sales teams are successful doing this cold-calling regiment.    Personally, I think that blanket cold calling takes a lot of time and is difficult to do on regular basis.   However, I do believe there is great value in walking into a prospective customer's office to introduce yourself in order to create more opportunity.

This is why I like the *Golden T*.  The *Golden T* is a simple procedure: every time you finish a sales appointment, you visit three surrounding businesses and introduce yourself.   Hence the shape of a *T*.   It's a strategic and effective method of door-to-door sales.

## THE GOLDEN T: 100% - DISCIPLINE

Let's say you just finished a great appointment with a prospective buyer, but instead of returning to your car, you quickly scan the area and stop into the three neighboring offices. You say, "I just was visiting Mr. Morrison next door about his shipping needs, and I wanted to come by and introduce myself to you."

This simple introduction can turn into a conversation about this person's shipping needs, getting you business right away, or into just a simple "Hello" that can build into a succession of "Hellos" and into a positive relationship that eventually nets you business or a referral.

You can also collect this person's information and put him or her on your calling sphere. And with *Golden T* visits, you and your prospects have a face to remember and an introduction to set the tone and basis for future calls: "Hello, Marge, you may remember my visiting you last week after I concluded business with your neighbor, Homer..."

## STOPPING BY THE BASES

One of the greatest things about the *Golden T* is you have a reason to be there. Since you are already meeting with the company next door, you are not randomly showing up to someone's office, a surprise which can put you and your prospect in an uncomfortable position and lead to an uncomfortable conversation for both parties.

> The Golden T gives you a positive reason to be in the neighborhood.

The *Golden T* provides you with an introduction that washes away any potential feelings of discomfort. When you say you are just in the neighborhood, you really are just in the neighborhood. And not for any reason, but because a neighbor of your prospect is doing business *with you.*

In short, you have a credible reason to be there and a reason that establishes your credibility. Unless you are late for your next appointment, why couldn't you visit three neighboring businesses?

## FEEL THE BOOST

Another great thing about the *Golden T* is that it is time effective. Since you are already at the building on an appointment, you do not have to do any extra driving or spend time looking up a phone number, address, or making a call ahead of time. You are there, and all you have to do is walk in the door.

It helps, of course, to schedule a little time between appointments so you have a moment for a quick introduction. You don't want to be late to your next appointment because you performed the Golden T, but then, you shouldn't leave the opportunity in the dust.

## WHAT THE GOLDEN T IS NOT

Let's be sure to separate ourselves from salespeople we sometimes call *the picture people*, *the speaker people* and *the plant people*. Who are these salespeople? You probably know them. They walk into someone's office and introduce themselves *with a lie*: "We just delivered some picture to a company down the street, and we have some left over pictures (plants, speakers, etc) that we will give you for pennies on the dollar." What they're peddling are knock-offs and maybe stolen merchandise.

It is important to note that these salespeople are not performing the *Golden T*. They are trying to make a few extra bucks on a whim and with a lie. Practitioners of the *Golden T*, on the other hand, are seeking long term relationships with prospects that lead to future business. Whereas speaker people just want to unload their speakers, *Golden T* practitioners want to invest in relationships and gain business for the future. The former engage in a gimmick; the latter invest in a serious enterprise.

## A GOLDEN DEMEANOR

> We are 100% energy. Make sure your energy is 100% golden!

It is critical to always be professional, truthful and polished. Your prospects will know if you are otherwise. There's no sense in making a poor first impression. At the same time, don't be so proud and arrogant that you think you are too good to cold call.

Have a golden demeanor, a shining attitude, when you do the Golden T. As I've said a lot in these pages, we are energy, and the Golden T presents us with a fantastic opportunity to transfer positive energy to new people.

## TAKING THE STEPS

The hardest part of the *Golden T* is doing it. Yeah, it makes sense and increases sales, but like most prospecting, it is not normally fun and can be scary. I've had the experience myself of getting ready to walk into an office and beginning to tell myself all the reasons why I should not take the step forward—they are not going to be there, maybe the door will be locked anyhow, they probably don't need my services, and so on.

The *Golden T* can be like asking the pretty girl to dance: you don't know if she will say "Yes" until you ask, but if you don't ask, you are guaranteed not to get the dance. The rejection can sting, but few experiences are as wonderful as the sound of her replying, "I would love to dance, thank you," not to mention the dance itself.

## WHAT IS YOUR BATTING AVERAGE?

Let's do the math: If we go on ten appointments per week, and we *Golden T* three companies for each appointment, and only one out of every six actually talk to us, we have gained five new prospects. Let's assume only one out of those five prospects actually do business with us; we still gain one new additional client per week!

> Simple math shows us the benefits of the Golden T.

The *Golden T* is not rocket science, nor is it necessarily fun (although I have had fun with it too), but like most things in life, the more you do it, the better and more comfortable you will be going it. Like all the practices I've discussed in this book, the *Golden T* isn't just something you can do; it is a skill you can master through repetition and – don't forget – through practice.

## WHAT IS YOUR HANDICAP?

Don't lie. There is nothing more damaging to the sales profession than those reps that use sneaky tactics and lie to get in the door.

I remember one day I was in my office and this young man and woman came in saying they were there to see the office manager. The man said he had an appointment scheduled to discuss their office supplies. I told them that I was the owner and didn't remember setting an appointment with them or even talking to them.

He should have taken the hint and stopped lying, but like a fool he continued, "Well, since we are here, can we talk to you about your office supplies?"

If you're lying to get an appointment, you are NOT doing the Golden T.

I candidly asked him if this cold-calling scam worked. He admittedly said it worked pretty well—sometimes.

I sarcastically congratulated him on his successes with the scam, but gave him my unsolicited advice: Don't ever lie to someone to get the appointment; sales is based on trust, and you lost the trust with your opening lie to me. You may gain some short-term clients, but you will lose in the long run. I wished him luck, although he didn't need it; he was already well on his way to being a professional and shameless con man. He was not, however, on the road to professional salesmanship.

If you are a sales professional, you don't need gimmicks and lies to find prospects. You just need the discipline and the focus. *You just need to prospect.*

## THE BOTTOM LINE

The *Golden T* is where time management and old school prospecting meets new school selling. A sales professional is able to maximize his or her time by using the windshield time from a current appointment to cold call three businesses, thus paving the way for a high success rate of getting a prospect's contact information and a possible personal endorsement from a current client. So don't let the next appointment you go on end with that one customer, let it be the beginning of three new prospects, and maybe your next customer.

## CHAPTER ELEVEN HIGHLIGHTS

- You can turn every one of your appointments into three new opportunities.

- *The Golden T* is time effective.

- It gives you a reason to be there.

- It takes discipline to walk in.

# 12

# THE APPOINTMENT

Ap·point·ment (ə-'p int-mənt) n. 1. *An arrangement to do something or meet someone at a particular time or place*

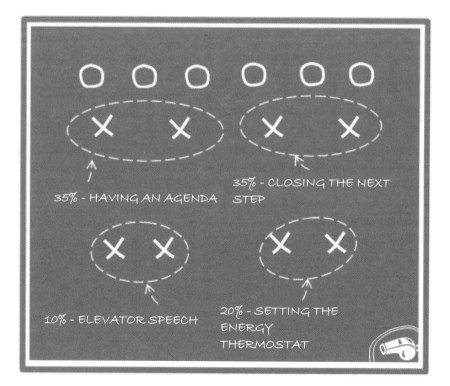

Before going on a sales call, it is vitally important that a sales professional is prepared.   I mean *fully* prepared, like a professional football player would be prepared for the Super Bowl or a shopaholic for Black Friday.

A sales professional needs to have company information about the people he or she is meeting, an agenda, and a list of purposeful questions.  The sales professional must absolutely have scrimmaged the call with a coach or team member prior to the appointment. *Don't go to the game without your glove and helmet or without having practiced!*

## WHAT ABOUT THE INFO?

With today's technology it is easier than ever to get company information as well as information about your contact.  By using RSS feeds, Google searches, LinkedIn, Facebook and other social media and information systems, you can find out more information about a company or person than you ever needed or wanted to know.

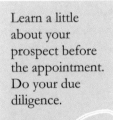

Learn a little about your prospect before the appointment. Do your due diligence.

Caution for all you research gurus: don't go to your appointment and start reciting the history of the account, quoting every press release the company has ever had, telling the contact about all his or her family history or complimenting a high school picture from classmates.com.

If you do any of those things, you'll come off as a creepy know-it-all or someone who is trying too hard to get business.  The prospective customer will start to wonder if you're a stalker or a wannabe Glenn Close from *Fatal Attraction*.  And don't even think about "befriending" the prospect on Facebook before an appointment.  That's certified stalker territory, there.

Do your research on the company and the contact, but don't share everything you discover.  Mention just enough to show you took the time to do your due diligence.  What you mention should serve as a touchstone on which the contact can step on and speak. People love to talk about themselves and their company. Give them that opportunity.

## PREPARATION: 35% - HAVING AN AGENDA

When preparing for the actual appointment, it is crucial to have an agenda—a *real* agenda. This agenda needn't change from appointment to appointment: it may vary a bit depending on circumstances, such how many calls it takes for you to close the sale, but overall it is a solid outline of your appointment. It's a formula to follow. Here is a sample:

*Appointment Agenda*

- Introduction
- Brief description of your company
- Learning and understanding about your prospect's company
- Seeing if there may be a good fit (remember: there may not always be a good fit)
- Closing the sale or scheduling the next step

You'll notice this agenda is very basic, yet gives you the road map for every stage of the appointment. Everything you do and say during the appointment fits into this agenda. Just be sure to say and do things at the appropriate time. You don't want to investigate a good fit before you've explained yourself and your company and inquired into your prospect and your prospect's company.

Do you find that you say things at the wrong time? Put stages in the wrong order? Well, scrimmage the appointment before the appointment. Practice the agenda before you put it into action.

## Have Your Play sheet with You

In a previous chapter we discussed coming up with your purposeful questions; when preparing for your appointment you should print these, take them with you, and *use* them. Do not rely on your memory or your brain. How many times have you said, "Oh man, I should have done X!" when you left an appointment?

I am a pen and pad guy; I take my questions with me, but I use a pen and pad to take notes—lots of notes. Those of you that have twenty-five yellow pads with notes from your past fifty appointments—you—yes, you—still need to print and take your questions with you.

> You lose nothing by bringing your questions with you, but you may lose the sale by not having them at hand.

Think about this for a second; what does it hurt to have your questions in hand, ready to reference so that they help keep you focused, on task, and prepared?

Sure, some would say that what makes sales professionals great is their ability to talk with a natural flow and the capacity to come up with things right on the spot—to be a "natural born" sales professional, as they say. If this has been used to describe you; don't believe your own press. However "natural" words come to you, you can always improve your game with questions right before you. Not doing so doesn't help you any, but having them available very well may. Why not crack the book at an open-book test?

While I've been guilty of winging the appointments without written questions and, admittedly, believing my own press, the more I stick to the basics and not rely on my wit to overcome any perceived lack of structure, *the more sales I win.*

## If You Don't Show Up for Practice, You Don't Get to Play

Sales professionals hate to role-play, yet it is absolutely necessary. That's why I wrote a whole chapter on it and why it's been an underlying theme throughout this whole book. Stop rolling your eyes and open your mind. If you or your children, grandchildren, nieces, nephews (and so forth) played any kind of competitive sports as a child, you know that you practiced more than you played. Even debate teams, spelling teams, teams of any kind *practice* before they compete. Actors and actresses practice before the performance. Even the Oscar winners. Especially the Oscar winners.

I starred in a play and in a big screen movie production (as an extra), and I can tell you from experience that actors practice. I was the starting quarterback for the division title game when in 8th grade. (I wish I could talk about high school or college ball, but by 9th grade I will still only 5'3"). So I can also tell you that 8th graders practice like mad. We scrimmaged every Wednesday before our games on Thursday. If Hill Country Middle School took scrimmaging seriously, professionals definitely can take it seriously.

Professional football teams scrimmage the day before a game and lawyers do mock trials to prepare for real upcoming trials. So, why not do the same for every sales call?

Sales professionals fall into the trap of thinking that the sales call is the only fun of their job, just like athletes sometimes think that playing the game is the only good part; it is not. The best part is playing, yes, but the second best part, what is almost as fun, is scrimmaging.

> Your intent determines whether you are role-playing or scrimmaging.

Hate to role-play? Then don't role-play— *scrimmage.* You may be thinking that all we are doing is changing a name, that nothing is really different. The difference *is the intent.* The intent of scrimmaging is to practice, whereas the intent of role-playing is usually to be evaluated.

Have you ever role-played in front of your peers and felt that you were being judged? That is role-playing, not scrimmaging. Some leaders and sales professionals use role plays to show how good they are or what they know, or worse what they don't know.

The intent of scrimmaging (practicing) is to prepare for the sales call (the fun stuff).  In short, if you like closing sales and making money, then scrimmage, and you will get it done.

## REVIEW YOUR PLAYS

When you meet with your prospective customers, pull out the agenda and show them how you plan on maximizing their time.    This also gives you a chance to ask prospects if there is anything they had in mind that they would like to add to the agenda.   At this point they may also interrupt you and say, "I am very busy, please get to the point."

Several years ago, when I was selling pagers, I went on an appointment, and the moment I got there the prospect half-heartedly shook my hand, said he didn't have much time, to please come in and make it quick.   Like most sales reps, I said no problem and hustled into his office.   Once again he said he really didn't have much time, that I could skip the BS and get right to the point.   He showed me what he had, what he was paying and asked me to quickly outline what I had and how much.

> Sell more than your product or service: sell YOU!

I did what a lot of us have done: I starting to try and ask questions. He gave me short answers and just kept asking, *how much*? So I ended up asking only a few questions before telling him about my company and our pricing.

He assured me that, yes, our pricing was cheaper than what he had and that he would get back to me. He thanked me for my time.

As you might expect, during my follow up call, he told me that his current provider matched the pricing I had given him, so there was no reason to change.

After experiencing this situation several more times (I can be a slow learner), I decided to do something about it. I practiced.  I asked a mentor and peer to practice my sales calls with me and I used this example. I knew it was important to have an agenda, and to share it, I just needed to learn how I could show my value, the importance of my time too (our time is just as important as the prospect's) and still close the sale.

A few years later, after years of steady scrimmaging, I went on an appointment with a sales professional on my team. We got to the appointment, and the contact said, nicely but straight to the point, "I am glad you are here, but I don't have a lot of time, so let's get right to it."

I responded to the prospect with a very sincere and confident voice: "Ms. Johnson, I can appreciate your schedule and time, but for us to make sure we do you adequate service and also make sure that this partnership is a good fit, we will need around 50 minutes and possibly several follow up appointments. So if this is not a good time, would it be possible to reschedule for a time that is better?"

> Your time is just as valuable as your prospect's. Be open about the time that you need to do your job.

At first she was a little shocked; however, I did not challenge her authority. On the contrary, I showed respect for her and reminded her that our time was important as well. She responded that it was not a problem and that she could move her schedule a bit. So we backed up, relaxed, started talking about our families and then discussed the agenda. As a result, we closed this sale.

## PREPARATION: 20% - SETTING THE THERMOSTAT

When you show up to an appointment or a customer walks in your front door, what is the temperature? I don't mean the temperature of the room or the physical temperature of the people. I mean the temperature of the energy in the room, the temperature you gauge without a thermometer.

Remember: we are energy, and when we interact with people we transfer that energy. If you read the chapter on likability, you know what I am talking about. Before you can even walk into the door of a prospective client's office, store or conference room, set your *energy thermostat* to max. Not over-the-top, manufactured, fake and annoying energy. I mean the energy that shows you are happy and makes being around you feel good.

In our homes the thermostat determines the temperature in the room, and the thermostat has to balance between the variables of temperature outside and the desired temperature in the room. The same can be said of our energy. If we meet with someone whose mood is poor, whose energy is low, then we may begin to feel the same way. The reverse is true as well. Display a sincerely good mood and show positive energy, and you transfer that energy and mood.

"Sales are contingent upon the attitude of the salesman, not the attitude of the prospect."

- W. Clement Stone

If your mood is high and energy is cranked up, then the chances of you closing the sale rise with the temperature. Your ability to close the sale will rise and fall with your energy thermostat. Everyone wants to feel good and be happy, so set your temperature accordingly before you even say hello.

## PREPARATION: 10% - ELEVATOR SPEECH

When going over the agenda, it is important to start with a brief introductory speech, something along the lines of, "I would like to tell you a little about our company and then ask you some questions so I can learn about you and your company. Would that be ok with you?"

It should take not any longer than an elevator ride to deliver this speech. Here are a couple of my old elevator speeches:

Comprehensive Financial Services: We are Comprehensive Financial Services; we specialize in life and health insurance. We help people save money for retirement and education while protecting their families. We have been working with clients in the state of Indiana for over 10 years.

Mobile Comm Paging: I am with MobileComm paging and we are a nationwide paging company that offers the latest technology in the paging industry. We help companies with their alphanumeric paging needs so that you can always be in contact when you need to be, to whom you want to be.

What is your "elevator speech"? Keep it short (less than 30 seconds).

_____

_____

_____

## PREPARATION: 35% - CLOSING THE NEXT STEP

Recall what I said about influential selling in the earlier chapters. Good energy, genuine interest, and confidence lead to likeability. Building trust is about asking the right questions in the right way. Influence requires a successful transition from asking questions to offering solutions and answers while, at the same time, establishing the value of oneself and one's company.

Once you have gone through all of the positions of Influential Selling – likeability, trust and influence – it is time to bring it home.

*Every appointment should have a close.* A real close that ensures there is a next step. During the chapter on consideration, I shared with you a bit about closing, but I want to touch on it again.

## WHAT IS THE SCORE

Have your closing statement in front of you. At the end of your appointment you should be able to say (a) I have contract, (b) I have follow-up appointment or (c) they said "No." By the way, you telling the prospect that you will follow up in a couple weeks is *not* an appointment; having a scheduled meeting or call next Wednesday at 2:00 pm *is*.

Sales professionals tell me all the time that they don't ask for the sale because it sounds "too salesy." My question is: why are you there, then? If what you sell helps people or companies, and you believe you are a fit, then ask them to let you help them! You're a sales professional; the prospects expect you to sound "salesy." They also expect you to be professional.

So be professional. It's what *really* matters.

## CHAPTER TWELVE HIGHLIGHTS

- A sales professional must be prepared.

- Be wary of the research guru syndrome.

- Have and bring an agenda.

- Share your agenda.

- Have and bring your questions.

- Prepare an elevator speech.

- Set your energy thermostat to max.

- Ask for the sale if you have earned it.

# POST-GAME COMMENTS

I hope you enjoyed this book and that you were able to take some ideas and processes out to help you to increase your sales. I take our profession very seriously, and I am proud to say I am a sales professional. Just like you, I know as long as I stay committed to learning and improving, I will always have a job.

Our job is to create revenue in organizations, and thousands of people rely on us to provide the revenue, which in turn provides for their families. But we must also realize that we cannot take ourselves too seriously because, after all, we are sales professionals.

In our world we must call people that sometimes don't want to talk to us, and we must go out and earn our paycheck (commission) every day.

Sales is a job that is truly based on our efforts and results. What we do is not a mere task, and it takes a lot more than product and industry knowledge. We must be able to find our clients, understand them, earn their trust, and at all costs be true to our word. Because in sales you are only as good as your last sale, and you will only make the next sale by doing the last one right.

As sale professionals we must help people and organizations make some of the most important of decisions, so take pride in your profession, and most of all, have fun doing it.

My name is Nathan Jamail, and I look forward to hearing about your future success.

# Index

## ABOUT THE AUTHOR

For the past decade Nathan Jamail has either been setting sales records, or training others on how to do so. As President of Jamail Development Group, as well as a small business owner himself, Nathan trains, coaches, and mentors sales professionals in many industries. Previously, Nathan set record results in sales by producing top performing sales teams in various capacities including business sales, direct consumer sales, indirect sales, distribution and marketing for several Fortune 100 companies. He has helped develop other executive leaders within Fortune 100 companies, small business owners, and individuals into successful coaches too.

Nathan's passion, energy and leadership have become the center of his success and those around him. He is known as an invincible sales leader with the ability to take the lowest producing areas of the country and build exemplary sales teams. The motto in which he lives by is: "If you BELIEVE, you will ACHIEVE." He implements this principle in businesses and organizations throughout the country. By teaching executive leaders that their number one asset is their employees, companies have seen higher levels of success.

As a practitioner and coach of sales and leadership, Nathan understands that a professional sales person or sales leader cannot be successful with a positive mental attitude alone. He teaches, and more importantly believes, that it takes a great balance of attitude, belief, skill, coaching, and practice to maximize one's skills and attributes for success. Based upon Nathan's firsthand experience, clients and organizations are able to identify challenges, maximize employee strengths, and increase productivity. His coaching and training programs have helped organizations increase their productivity up to and over 300%!

Nathan has been featured and interviewed by Fox Television and various other publications regarding his leadership style and the success that he has created. He is the author of *The Sales Leaders Playbook* and the *Sales Leaders Workbook*.

## NATHAN JAMAIL'S MOST REQUESTED TOPICS

✪ Building and Leading Winning Teams
*"How to create and sustain performance"*

✪ Influential Selling
*"Create referrals by creating relationships"*

✪ Team Work of Art Teambuilding and Workshops
*"Creatively bringing teams together"*

---

Nathan Jamail, a sought after keynote and motivational speaker is available for your next workshop, meeting, and seminar.

Book him for your next event by contacting your favorite speaker's bureau or log onto www.nathanjamail.com

---

What people are saying:

*"Nathan is a high energy individual and it makes the message more believable when you can see that this guy knows how to be successful. Nathan took a lot of time to learn about our organization and tailor his remarks for our benefit. I would certainly recommend him to any group with new or experienced managers."*

*Marvin Mutchler*
*First Savings Bank*
*President/CEO*

*"Nathan is one of the strongest sales professionals that I've worked with over the past 12 years. In my opinion, his success is based on his ability to motivate people as well as the ability to teach and train people on the fine art of selling and customer behavior. I highly recommend Nathan Jamail"*

Charles Moore
Metro PCS
Staff VP, Finance and Operations

*"He is a phenomenal motivational speaker, captivating his audiences and engaging them in discovering and developing their skills and talents, allowing them to accelerate in their personal growth. I would strongly recommend Nathan and encourage anyone who values building and developing their sales teams to benefit from his professional services."*

Craig Walter
Radio Shack
Senior VP, Consumer Market

*"My agents have expressed how much Nathan's training has helped them to better approach their clients and close more sales. Nathan's training has positively impacted this company. I look forward to your continued support and welcome future trainings. I highly recommend Nathan"*

Linda Reed
Fenwick Realtors
Vice President

You can also request information by sending an email to:
info@nathanjamail.com.

"I look forward to your future success!" -- *Nathan Jamail*

# THE PLAYBOOK ORDER FORM

☐ Yes, I want _____ copies of *The Sales Professional's Playbook* at $24.95 each (plus $3.49 shipping per book). Please allow 14 business days for delivery. Texas residents please add $2.06 sales tax per book. International orders must be paid by credit card or accompanied by a postal money order in U.S. funds. Please add $7 shipping per book.

☐ My check or money order for $_____ is enclosed.

☐ Please charge my: ☐ Visa ☐ MasterCard

Card #: _____

Expiration Date: _____ Security Code: _____

Signature: _____

Name: _____

Organization: _____

Shipping Address: _____

_____

City/State/Zip: _____

Phone: _____

Email: _____

Billing Address (if different): _____

City/State/Zip: _____

Please make check or money order payable to:
Jamail Development Group
2591 Dallas Parkway Ste 300
Frisco, TX 75034

*You can also purchase online at:* **www.nathanjamail.com**

Facebook: http://www.facebook.com/jdgroup

Twitter: **http://twitter.com/#!/nathanjamail**